G000230976

Secu

&

Last Scrapings

Second Helpings
& *Last Scrapings*

Simon Brown

MARBLE HILL ❧ LONDON

This expanded edition including
Last Scrapings first published in 2023 by
Marble Hill Publishers Ltd
Flat 58 Macready House
75 Crawford Street
London W1H 5LP

www.marblehillpublishers.co.uk

Second Helpings first published in 2021 by
Marble Hill, London

A CIP catalogue record for this book is available from the British Library.

ISBN 978 1 7392657 2 4

EXPANDED EDITION

Typeset in Adobe Caslon Pro 10/14 pt

Printed and bound by Ingram Spark

Design by Dan Brown

THIS VOLUME IS PRINCIPALLY FOR MY *lovely wife, Jenny. It is also for my family and friends generally, including particularly all those who wrote to me so generously after reading the earlier memoir, with kind words of approval and encouragement, words which greatly enhanced the long months of lockdown which followed. Indeed, wider still and wider, I dedicate this further volume to all who go out of their way in life to cheer their fellow beings with words of praise and goodwill. The world would be a happier place if, in life generally, tributes were more widely splashed about. The governing rule should be: if in doubt admire; condemn only if you must.*

ACKNOWLEDGEMENTS

In the course of writing this volume
I regularly consulted an editorial circle
of five. If there are more enthusiastic
publishers than Francis Bennett, more
talented book designers than son, Dan,
subtler critics than Richard Johnson
and other son, Ben, let alone more
forbearing wives than Jenny, I have yet
to meet them. I am inexpressibly grateful
to them all.

Contents

Second Helpings

Last Scrapings

Introduction

C LOSING MY MEMOIR *Playing off the Roof & Other Stories,*
I expressly contemplated (threatened?) the possibility of a further
volume, *Second Helpings.* Well, here it is, and bearing that very title,
an accurate indication of its essential nature: more of the same. It
is, in short, a collection, positively a liquorice allsorts mixture, of
stories, reminiscences, reflections, one or two notable legal cases
revisited, ending (as did the earlier volume) with a lecture, this
one given in 2010 on the pros and cons of trial by jury, but this one
introduced in a separate chapter rather than being simply annexed.

It is of course in the earlier memoir that will be found the basic
story of my life, its successive stages described, these the context for
the various anecdotes and reminiscences recounted. Such being the
case this further volume, unless perhaps acquired as a taster, is most
likely to appeal to those who enjoyed the original. And certainly it
it is with the original that I would urge new readers to start.

That said, for anyone who acquires this volume without having
read the earlier memoir, and with no prior knowledge whatever of
my life and career, I had better include a brief paragraph or two
summarising these.

After a fairly conventional middle-class early life (father at war in Burma, boarding school for me at seven), I did two years' National Service in the gunners, went to Oxford to read history, changed whilst there to law, and was called to the Bar in 1961. I had a general common law practice until 1979 when I was appointed Treasury Counsel (acting thereafter solely for the Crown). In 1984 I became a High Court (Queen's Bench) judge, in 1992 a Lord Justice of Appeal (Court of Appeal), and in 2004 a Law Lord. In 2009 the Law Lords were re-created as a new UK Supreme Court and there I remained until reaching the mandatory retirement age of seventy-five in 2012. Since then I have regularly attended the House of Lords as a working crossbench peer.

I would like to say that I have written this further volume simply to satisfy the cravings of those who, not yet replete, urged me to write more (and certainly some, flatteringly, did just that). But the fact is that I so enjoyed writing the original memoir, and so relished the many happy memories it brought back, that, as further recollections came to mind, and the enforced idleness of the Covid lockdown provided the opportunity, I succumbed to the temptation to start afresh, albeit this time serving up rather smaller portions, as surely befit second helpings.

Mostly, but not invariably, these new pieces appear in roughly chronological order. But each is really self-standing and they can be read in whatever order takes the reader's fancy. Perhaps they can be regarded as missing pieces from the earlier volume. But more realistically they are just additional stories, intended at least as much to amuse as to inform.

A footnote: *Playing off the Roof*, a snappy title as I thought, had the tiresome consequence of initially being found listed in Amazon's DIY construction section. *Second Helpings*, I hope, won't end up in the Cookery list.

CHAPTER I

National Service Revisited

IT'S ODD HOW one's time in National Service, now over sixty years ago, still occasionally comes back to mind, perhaps because it was all so very different from everything that followed.

First, a memory from my time at Mons OCTU (Officer Cadet Training Unit), an army camp in the outskirts of Aldershot. Being within easy reach of London, many cadets spent their nights in town instead of polishing brass, blancoing belts and bulling boots. Mostly these were the cavalrymen (though of course destined then for tanks not horses) rather than unfashionable gunners like myself. But one night in particular I recall, though rather for the aftermath than for the evening itself. The evening I spent at a debutantes' ball, one of a number of such events to mark the coming out of a second cousin, one of the Salmon and Gluckstein girls, held that night in County Hall, Westminster.

County Hall, a fine Edwardian baroque building with magnificent public rooms fronting the river just south of Westminster Bridge, then housed the LCC, in those years chaired by Col Sir Louis Gluckstein QC MP (known to all as Luigi), a towering figure, both physically and metaphorically, the recognised head of his illustrious family. The disintegration of J. Lyons & Co, the family business and, though unconnected, the privatisation of County Hall on its abolition as the seat of London government, all in the 1980s, were two of the more depressing events of those times. All that, however, is for present purposes entirely by the way.

The evening over, I unfortunately, if all too predictably, missed the last train back to Aldershot and had to wait for the milk train, returning just in time to change hurriedly from white tie into battle dress. But I was extremely tired. Not merely had I had no sleep that night but, as it happened, I'd had precious little the night before either. As ill-luck would have it, the previous night I had been on guard duty at the barracks, two hours on, two off, over a twelve-hour period. During the hours off one remained booted and in uniform, consigned to a hard bunk and issued with a rough blanket, conditions hardly conducive to deep sleep.

Although exhausted, I survived the morning drill session: it is not easy to doze whilst energetically square-bashing to the raucous commands of the CSM. The squad then repaired to an over-heated lecture room for an hour's instruction, I forget on what topic but plainly less than mesmerising. In the course of it I recall trying desperately to keep my eyes open. My next memory, however, is of the instructor waking me up and addressing me directly, and my finding that even then I was powerless to stay awake.

One reads of soldiers in warfare fighting hand to hand even after two or three days without sleep. That I find astounding. Perhaps had the lecturer actually been trying to bayonet or shoot me I might just have managed to keep my eyes open. Certainly, however, that morning it was beyond me. On I slept, waking again only as the lecture finally ended.

The incident was reported to my company commander. Happily he took a relaxed view of the matter and my punishment was merely to be gated (confined to barracks) for a fortnight. For those weeks the London season had to manage without me. I have no recollection of any debutante's heart being broken on that account.

≈

AS DESCRIBED IN my original memoir, after being commissioned from Mons and a spell with my new regiment in Essex, we were posted abroad. Almost immediately after sailing we were notified that, instead of going to Malta, we were instead destined for Cyprus, as part of the force engaged in the Suez adventure. At that point it became part of my task to censor the men's mail to ensure they gave no hint of where in truth we were now secretly bound. I confess to having learned in the process more about the anatomical possibilities of the sexual act than I had previously dreamed of.

After describing graphically what he looked forward to doing with his beloved when next they met, one man added: "…and if it weren't that this letter is going to be read by some snotty-nosed young officer, I'd tell you what I'd really like to do to you!"

My imagination boggled.

≈

ONCE FINALLY we arrived in Cyprus we spent a nightmarish week in a transit camp just outside Nicosia and then established ourselves in tented accommodation near Limassol, remaining under canvas for the further eight months or so of our stay on the island.

For whatever reason, on arrival I found myself appointed mess officer, with responsibility not least for keeping a well-stocked bar. No one ever questioned my success in this: we had limitless barrels of beer, crates of wine and every spirit and liqueur known to man. Not an officer in the regiment was able, though many tried, to start an evening's drinking at one end of the liqueur shelf and, sampling all between, reach the other end still standing. So the stocking of the bar was really not a problem. But regrettably the paying for it was.

We ran this tented mess on a self-service, honour-based, system: whoever took a drink had to sign for it. Quite why there was no barman, I forget; perhaps there was simply a shortage of mess staff. Now I have little doubt that honour did indeed prevail and that all duly signed the mess book for every drink they took. But alas we had no measures as such and, after a while, it became ever clearer that people's idea of a measure was becoming increasingly elastic, particularly as the evenings wore on. Not to put too fine a point on it, after the first month the bar account was found to be very substantially in deficit.

Reporting this to the colonel, I was immediately struck by how seriously he took it. Naive as I was, I had rather supposed he would accept it as just one of those things, an understandable consequence of our unusual new situation. Somehow I had failed to realise that accurate fund-accounting is regarded as an absolute imperative in the Services. I was, I confess, considerably shaken when words such as "court-martial" began to enter the conversation.

To cut the story short, however, the colonel (with whom, those familiar with my earlier memoir may recall, I had used occasionally to play golf when we were stationed in Essex) proved in truth to be a kindly, understanding and forgiving figure. With his support I was allowed to arrange a whip-round amongst the officers to make good the shortfall. A mess orderly was found, together with some measuring devices. But, unsurprisingly, a new mess officer was appointed in my place.

I was in short spared all punishment; unless, that is, my new appointment as the regimental MTO (Motor Transport Officer) was to be so characterised. That certainly was how I personally regarded it. I took no interest whatever in military vehicles and never understood the workings of an internal combustion engine and for that matter still don't. But, as so often in army life, my sergeant knew it all and kept me out of further trouble. I left the bonnet-opening to him.

ぶ

MY FINAL ARMY REMINISCENCE dates from our return home from Cyprus in the spring of 1957, stationed back in Essex. A film was being made of *Dunkirk*, starring John Mills and Richard Attenborough. This was the only occasion in my life I ever witnessed, let alone took part in, a film. Ours was one of three regiments bussed down to Camber Sands on the south coast to be blown up on the beaches, Basically we had to lie down in the sand whilst small explosive devices were detonated all around us. When the following year I saw the film I was quite unable to identify myself in it, but that is immaterial. All that I recall of our two or three days on the coast whilst the beach scenes were shot is a drinks party we held for the stars in our (once again tented) mess. It took place during a torrential rainstorm and John Mills alone of the stars turned up, a courteous gesture we all felt.

We now move on some thirty years to Denham Golf Club, where John Mills (by then knighted and living alongside the course) and I were both members. Delightful though he was, he was not a particularly gregarious member and he had an all too well deserved reputation as the slowest golfer in the club. Generally he played with his wife and they held up the entire course. One summer afternoon, having followed him painfully slowly around a largely empty course, I eventually found myself next to him in the club bar.

Although usually respectful of his privacy, having had to wait to play every shot in the round, I felt justified in engaging him in light conversation. It had been, I said, some years since we had last met but we were once in the same film together. He looked at me somewhat quizzically whilst obviously racking his brains trying to remember who on earth this erstwhile fellow thespian could possibly be. But he quickly then turned on his Oscar-winning smile as I told him the same rather thin story I've just told you. He was, I may say, delighted with it. I'm less confident that you, dear reader, will be.

CHAPTER 2

Oxford Encore

W HEN TO MY great delight, some five years ago, my eldest granddaughter, Minnie (Jess to most), was accepted for Oxford, I immediately gave her the only piece of advice I thought necessary.

Don't, I said, make the mistake I made. Don't fritter away the mornings, staying in bed late, meeting for coffee, chatting with friends or just wandering around the bookshops. Have a good breakfast at 9 and then work solidly for three hours, 10–1. That will put you ahead of the game and the rest of the day will be yours to do with as you wish.

Minnie looked at me hard, her mother (Jenny junior, Ben's wife, now head of the City of London School for Girls) harder still. Nobody these days, they insisted, can survive Oxford on less than eight hours' work a day, more like ten on essay days. Goodness, how different things were in the late 1950s.

Many are the accounts of undergraduate life in times past (a few lyrical, too many hackneyed). Most of those lucky enough to have entered the portals of that enchanted city have the happiest of memories: of exciting new friends, of passionate love affairs (alas, generally short-lived and unconsummated), of stimulating clubs and societies, of absorbing lectures, of intense and challenging debates, of vividly recalled plays and films, operas and concerts, of exotic parties, of pubs, bars and butteries, of laughter, fun and chatter, chatter always and everywhere – in short the whole kaleidoscope of rich new experiences that crowd in upon receptive young minds.

ᔧ

MY EARLIER MEMOIR, insofar as it touched on Oxford, described only my admission interview, a disappointing tea party and changing schools from history to law. Still now I wonder if much else will interest even the most loyal of grandchildren. Will they think it amusing or merely odd that I went to not a single law lecture, attending instead only such compelling performances as were given by the undisputed showmen of the lecture halls: Isaiah Berlin, A. J. P. (Alan) Taylor, Hugh Trevor-Roper and the celebrated art historian, Edgar Wind.

Still less can I expect the grandchildren to take one tenth the same delight in hearing of my sporting activities as I took engaging in them. But nonetheless, if only "for the record", I proudly recall my captaincy of a Worcester Cuppers hockey team then boasting three current internationals (Mike Eagar for England, Hugh Cairns and Neil Livingston for Scotland), defeated only by the sportsmen's college, Teddy Hall. Squash too I played for the college and, this the brief pinnacle of my Oxford sporting life, once (alas, just the once) for the Squirrels, the University second five. I should perhaps in all honesty add that, taking a college team over to Stowe for a match, myself playing against their captain, Chris Atkinson, whom I had actually coached at the school as a promising new boy some five years earlier, I won merely a handful of points, a humbling reminder of my essentially only modest skill at the game.

During the summer terms I played college tennis midweek, cricket for the Rustics (Worcester's socially prestigious mixed ability team) against local clubs and villages most Sundays. As secretary of the Rustics (before becoming captain the next year), it was my task, first to ensure an acceptable balance between Americans (who had never played the game before but, baseball-trained, threw in brilliantly from the outfield and slogged the occasional six) and university cricket blues looking for relaxation – and, second, to ensure a sufficient number of our team had cars for transport.

Sport, in short, was an important part of my life at Oxford and the source of many lasting friendships. But I hugely regret never having been close enough to blues standard in any of them to be eligible for election to Vincent's, the one club of which I have always regretted not being a member, if only to wear their instantly recognisable tie (navy blue with silver crowns) that so regularly and enviably adorns the neck of so many old friends, Michael Beloff, Robin Butler and Colin Mackay amongst them.

Before finally closing this digression into sport, I add only that Rustics cricket prepared me admirably for the only team sport I ever played in the years that followed, an annual Sunday cricket match between the Islington Incompetents and the Gentlemen of Buckinghamshire.

The fixture was begun originally by rival brothers-in-law and played first at the Dashwood (Hellfire Caves) Estate at West Wycombe and later at Mentmore Towers, both wonderful grounds where we joyfully assembled mid-morning with our Volvos, our wives and children, our picnic hampers, and our barrels of this, magnums of that. For the last several years of the fixture, Bill Keegan was our captain, I the long-standing (in every sense) wicketkeeper. Somehow, to my great delight, Bill managed one year to slip this fact into one of his City Editor columns in the *Observer*, whether to illustrate the sturdy resilience of whatever practice he was discussing, or its essential unreliability, I no longer recall.

&

AS BUT A FOOTNOTE to this chapter I record one dismal omission from my Oxford life: never once did I take to the river, one of Oxford's most obvious attractions. Never once did I hire a rowing boat; never did I go punting, and indeed to this day I have never experienced the fabled delights of taking a girl, a picnic and a punt from Magdalen Bridge for long leisurely hours up the sun-dappled Isis river. Stupidly it became almost a point of pride for me not to engage in this most popular of university passtimes. And now perhaps I have left it too late even for my grandchildren to help close this most ridiculous gap in my experience.

Almost all the regrets one has in life are for things that one failed to do, not for the things that one actually did.

CHAPTER 3

Three Long Summers

SELDOM DO ONE's spirits rise when people bring out their holiday snaps. And in these volumes thus far I have assiduously avoided doing any such thing. Many foreign trips have featured but invariably connected to some aspect of my working life. As a family we have over the years been on a great number of enjoyable and interesting holidays abroad. But the reader will continue to be spared these. Except for this single chapter which records three long summer holidays spent in my early twenties, a most impressionable time of life. This chapter, I may say, has been urged upon me by my now similarly aged grandchildren, themselves perhaps hoping for similar chances to travel at leisure abroad.

❧

1957

THE SUMMER OF 1957, following two years' National Service, I spent mostly in New York, some eight weeks of it working by day as a "store-room clerk" stacking shelves in the basement of a fashionable Fifth Avenue goods shop, Black, Starr and Gorham (the Aspreys of New York), a job arranged in advance by my father.

To be allowed to work, I had first had to get an immigration visa, surprisingly easy in those days, culminating in a visit to a US lady consul in Regent Street who earnestly wished me well in my new life abroad. I hadn't the heart to tell her that I'd be back in England in some ten weeks' time.

I crossed the Atlantic in an aged Greek Line ship (the charge less than £50 for the return journey), sharing with two returning American students a dingy cabin well below the waterline. This accommodation contrasted sharply with that awaiting me on arrival, also arranged by my father. I stayed with a wealthy family (he a Wall Street lawyer, Simon Rose) out in Westchester County (Mamaroneck the local stop for the daily rail commute into Grand Central Station). They lived in some style. There was a Dufy in my bedroom, two Rouaults in the hallway, other impressionists elsewhere. There was also weekend tennis and swimming and almost nightly barbecues. (It was sweltering hot in New York, humidity downtown in the high nineties.) The whole family were charming and amongst their lively group of young friends was a pretty girl, tending to get paired off with me, Dawn Frost – though certainly not frosty and I doubt she ever saw the dawn.

After a month of this luxury, however, I decided to move into the city itself, certainly for midweek, to free myself for a more adventurous social and cultural life than was possible staying with family friends and commuting. To this end I found a cheap hotel (really a dosshouse) in central New York, charging just ten dollars a week, seemingly catering exclusively for the black population. Indeed I do not recall ever seeing another white person there throughout my stay. But naturally this was not of the slightest interest or concern for me, unlike probably many US citizens in those days when cases like *Brown v Board of Education* were the lead news stories.

Many happy memories I retain of those weeks in the city. Of a black-tie charity gala (as a guest of the Rose family) at the United Nations building with the entertainment provided by Benny Goodman (clarinettist) and his orchestra. Of an evening spent with a distant relation, a wealthy, good-looking, middle-aged divorcée living on Park Avenue. On my arrival she asked if I'd like to meet Alistair Cooke (of *Letter from America* fame) and, when naturally I assented, she phoned his apartment below and up he immediately came, entertaining us initially on the piano and then throughout dinner with a string of wonderful stories. The evening over, I stayed the night, only much later realising that my hostess's visit to bid me an affectionate goodnight had almost certainly been an intended seduction which I was still then too innocent to have recognised. I went to galleries, plays and operas. And I was taken to top league baseball and American football games. What it was to be young and fancy-free in that most vibrant and exuberant of cities.

From New York I went to Montreal to stay for a week with an army friend who had just emigrated there. Thence to Quebec and the voyage home.

1958

MY FIRST UNIVERSITY long vacation was planned with two friends: John Boulton, a fellow National Service officer who had then gone up to Cambridge, and (for part of the trip only) Tony Copley, Worcester's history scholar of our year, who had become a close friend though he saw me, rightly, as an uncommitted historian. They had not known each other before but met through me and got on well.

John and I were to make our way to Athens where we would

meet up with Tony and then spend some weeks travelling together around Greece and the islands before Tony went off to Mt Athos whilst John and I went on to Istanbul.

We were to travel light and as cheaply as possible. Rucksacks and lilos were all we carried and during the entire twelve weeks of the trip I recall paying for only three night's accommodation (at youth hostels in Istanbul and Brussels). Almost as soon as we left England my lilo developed a leak that I was never able to pinpoint and repair and it became entirely routine to have to reinflate it two or three times a night for the many weeks to come.

Other people's travelogues generally make for tedious reading so I shall chart our itinerary only very lightly.

Our first night was spent in a beach hut in Newhaven. Thence by the early morning ferry to Dieppe where we were lucky enough to hitch a lift with two young City swells in a fast convertible all the way to Nice (hitch-hiking was never remotely as easy again). Our next arranged stop was the Hotel Splendido at Portofino where John's sister, Julia, was honeymooning, and there we enjoyed our first shower and a sumptuous dinner before dossing down for the night in their dressing room. From there we progressed slowly to Naples where I had been provided with an introduction to our naval consul and his wife and once more luxury replaced the discomforts of life on the road.

After three days there we travelled on by sea, deck-class to Athens (Piraeus) where again we had arranged to stay with friends. These were the Page sisters: Anthea, whom John and I knew well from Cyprus days (nights) as the daughter of the regiment, and her exotic elder half-sister, Juanita. Here Tony joined us and it was here, as we later learned, that the Page sisters each made strenuous efforts to seduce him, only then discovering (as, indeed, later still did John and I) that Tony was gay – something that was going to cause him terrible trouble later in the year at Oxford and in his subsequent life as an academic, barring him from entry to the USA.

After a few days in Athens and a quick trip with the Pages to Mykonos, the three of us went briefly to Rhodes and Lindos (for the butterflies), then spent a month travelling first to Delphi and then around the Peloponnese, visiting all the usual classical sites. We ate almost nothing but Ogen melons, stuffed tomatoes and yoghurt (could one wish for more?), using the free olive oil to deepen our tans by frying in the sun. *Enosis* remaining a source of friction between Greece and the UK, we did once have to pretend to Dutch nationality when passing through a remote village. But overall these were carefree and happy days, eating at the humblest tavernas we could find and sleeping out in the fields, soon reconciled to waking daily with hands and faces covered in innumerable mosquito bites.

On return to Athens, our few clothes freshly laundered and our farewells made, John and I sailed, deckclass again, to Istanbul, that magical city with which we both instantly fell in love. Here too I had some family introductions and, in striking contrast to our youth hostel nights, we were on occasions lavishly entertained. Dined one evening by business associates of my father's at the Istanbul Hilton, embarrassingly unaware that the succession of succulent *meze* dishes which we greedily gorged with our drinks were but a prelude to the main menu, we needed all our willpower to do justice to the meal itself. Another evening was spent as guests of a distinguished politician with his wife and daughters at the fashionable Moda Beach Club annual summer black-tie Ball, for which they provided us with the necessary dinner jackets.

But unquestionably the outstanding, the abiding, memory of that first visit to Istanbul was of swimming the Bosphorus, from Europe to Asia, a feat of which I have boasted now for upwards of sixty years. John was a good swimmer, I an indifferent one, though supremely fit at the time. We decided to cross halfway between the city and the Black Sea where historic ruined Ottoman castles front either side and the Bosphorus is at its narrowest, only some half a mile across albeit its current therefore at its most vicious. The channel follows a serpentine course and, realising we were bound to be carried a little way downstream, we aimed to land at a point diagonally across just short of where it turned into a further bay.

Even in those days there was a good deal of water traffic so we set off at dawn having hired a small motorised fishing boat to carry our clothes and bring us back afterwards. In we dived and at once found that almost all our strength and energy had to be devoted to combating the current to avoid being swept miles downstream (the lengthy course taken by the hundreds who nowadays enter for the annual Bosphorus swim when it is officially closed for the day to shipping). John just managed to make it to the point diagonally opposite. I simply couldn't and, watching as the current inexorably took me past it, and recognising that I had no strength left to cross the bay now opening up on my left, I shouted out to our boatman for rescue. Much hope. I doubt he heard me. But whether he did or not he was altogether more intent on his next catch than on me. Finally, noticing the current start to slacken as gradually I came closer to the edge. I just managed to haul myself ashore. And there I lay, shattered but greatly relieved, for the fifteen minutes or so it took John to walk round and find me. The Dardanelles it is not and no Byron I, but, though at the time I saw it just as a youthful frolic, in retrospect I regard it as a truly heroic feat.

After Istanbul, John went back to Italy, I to Yugoslavia, sailing up the Adriatic, stopping at Korchula and Split and then on to Dubrovnik where, from sheer exhaustion, I fell asleep lying on a marble floor during a sellout concert by the Oistrachs, father and son.

After then spending a week in Venice and the historic towns just to the west, I met John again in Milan, hitch-hiking together from there over the Simplon and on eventually to Brussels where we stayed briefly for the World Fair before finally returning home.

We had been away for three months, totally out of touch with our families, spending under £100 in all (travel included), less than 10 shillings a day on sustenance. For the first time in my life I had (mostly) been living rough. I was proud of my beard (pictured in my earlier memoir). And of one thing I was quite sure: never again would an Oxford tea party leave me utterly bereft of conversation.

1959

ONE OF THE MOST sought-after jobs for one's final Oxford long vacation was to be a courier for Specialised Travel Service, a company run from Baker Street by a Mr Baum and a Mr Batsek, which took groups of American and Canadian students on summer tours around Europe. The job paid twenty-five shillings (equivalent now to some £30) a day and was all found (literally every last expense). The tours were most expertly arranged, the courier's tasks being, first, to carry all the tickets and vouchers (for all means of travel, plane, train, coach or whatever; for all accommodation; for every booked museum, ticketed place of worship or entertainment; for every guide, every meal, and anything else programmed in); secondly, to assign hotel rooms (usually doubles) to the tour members; and thirdly to organise and take care of the group generally. On the rare occasions when arrangements broke down, the courier had a discretionary fund to meet the needs of the hour.

Only Oxbridge undergraduates were employed as couriers and we were, indeed, ideal for the purpose: our standing and accents appealed to the tour members; many of us were already reasonably well travelled (though we were never ourselves required to act as guides); and those of us who had done National Service had the necessary organisational skills. And of course the job was ideal for us too: free, indeed paid, travel with plentiful sight-seeing and cultural trimmings.

I applied for the job and, following a rigorous interview in London, was accepted as courier for a tour of thirty Canadian university students, male and female, to start in London and then visit eight countries in eight weeks: Holland, Belgium, Luxembourg, Germany, Austria, Switzerland, Italy and France, ending in Paris.

It would be of no interest to rehearse the details of the tour programme. Suffice it to say we visited only the most obvious places, mostly the capital cities, and to pick out just the odd event which perhaps serves to distinguish this trip from the innumerable other such tours that take place every summer. Many stops included pre-arranged visits to specialist shops (for example those selling glass in Venice, leather in Florence). Here the tour guide would routinely be paid a hidden commission, generally fifteen percent of the total spend. I thought this quite wrong (an instinct which squared with what years later I learned to be the law condemning secret commissions) and, to the shopkeeper's invariable surprise, negotiated instead that each tour member would get a fifteen percent discount. But any goodwill I earned from this I certainly lost by what some of the group regarded as my overbearing manner in organising them. Timekeeping is obviously of some importance for the efficient functioning of such a tour: unless everyone is punctual in assembling for the tour coach or whatever, the majority are kept hanging about and the programme is plagued by delays. My habit was to bawl out the latecomers rather as in my National Service days. Unsurprisingly perhaps, this was resented.

Of the tour events I mention just one: a wonderful production of *Fidelio* at the East Berlin opera house (famous for its chocolate cake), travelling there by underground (this of course before the Wall was built). When, on becoming Treasury Devil some twenty years later, I was being positively vetted, I well recall being upbraided for having failed to disclose this brief excursion behind the Iron Curtain; I had of course completely overlooked it.

Scarcely less memorably, during our few days in Germany, one of the girls lost her passport in Munich the day before we were to leave for Vienna. Unfortunately it was a Sunday and I had to devote almost the entire day to procuring her an alternative travel document – only later to hear she'd subsequently found the passport whilst packing overnight, news that positively compounded my exasperation.

When the tour finally ended in Paris, I bade the group a fond farewell and the same day moved on to the next stage of my vacation. For this I had managed to persuade an Oxford friend to drive my car (still the Ford Popular I had so irresponsibly crashed during National Service) together with my girlfriend to meet up with me in Paris. He would then go his separate way whilst she and I would spend the next month driving around Spain.

I once began a judgment in the House of Lords, having noted that each of my four colleagues had already set out their views at length: "There is much to be said for my saying little, little to be said for my saying much", a sentence which delighted Alan Rodger who called it a perfect chiasmus (a categorisation later disputed by my son, Dan). At all events, it now seems to me an apt start to an account of a month spent touring Spain. There are surely more than enough descriptions of other such tours already. We went to all the obvious places and did all the obvious things. We ate sucking pig and *paella* and generally we drank too much. We swam and we sunbathed and we saw all the sights. Occasionally we bumped into university friends and that was fun. It was, in short, a glorious month and we loved it all. To describe it beyond that would, I believe, bore my readers stiff and so I leave it there.

Back to England we drove and my final year at Oxford began. It required rather more work than by then I was used to. But what a summer it had been.

CHAPTER 4

Dinners and Speakers

I HAVE WRITTEN already of Francis Reynolds as my law tutor and effectively he was. But strictly he was my junior tutor, a mere four years older than me who had himself only recently graduated from the college. So I should briefly mention too Worcester's senior law Fellow, A. B. (Alan) Brown, a cheerful Australian whose interest in undergraduates, certainly by the time of my arrival, had substantially waned. There was a real chance that he wouldn't actually appear at one's weekly tutorial and, generally to the relief of their authors, many essays went unread.

But A.B. played a notable role in Oxford's civic life, Mayor (an office later elevated to Lord Mayor) for many years, and a widely acclaimed after-dinner speaker, recognised by the toastmasters of England as matched only by the legendary Lord (Norman) Birkett. Formal dinners in those days boasted (if that is the word) four speakers. A.B. always insisted on the last slot. This enabled him to demonstrate his quite remarkable skill of extemporisation: his ability, with mere jottings from the earlier speeches on the back of his menu, ingeniously to weave these into a witty theme of his own. I witnessed this three times, each a tour de force.

Over the subsequent decades I have heard innumerable after-dinner speeches and indeed made a good few myself. But it is a mistake to suppose that all barristers and judges, simply because used to public speaking, possess this skill; indeed, only a very few have I wanted to hear a second time.

One such was Tom Bingham, a master in all he undertook. Speaking on behalf of the guests (of whom I was one) at an annual dinner of the solicitors' prestigious Justinian Club (the membership consisting of a single partner from each of the leading City law firms), held that year at the Cavalry Club, Tom began by saying he'd been musing for some time on our hosts' choice of venue until:

"It suddenly struck me that, of course, what the members of both clubs have in common is that they all charge ferociously."

❧

CONTINUING SUCH a list of outstanding speakers would be not merely invidious but likely to make me more enemies than friends. For every appointment, it is said, there are ten disappointments. So too for every list of best this or that.

I would, however, mention just one other, from times long past, a Jewish Old Bailey judge of the 1960s and '70s, Alan King-Hamilton QC. I mention him not only because he was a most accomplished speaker at City dinners (the source of one particular story well worth preserving to which I come later), but also because he produced my very favourite judicial witticism.

One of the better-known silks regularly defending at the Old Bailey in that era was Billy Rees-Davies, a rumbustious Tory MP who had lost an arm in the war, widely known to his fellow practitioners as "the one-armed bandit" (the name of a then prevalent gambling machine). In a rape trial one day before

King-Hamilton, Rees-Davies, not uncharacteristically bullying and mocking the somewhat tearful complainant, to the jury's evident displeasure, suddenly felt his gown tugged from behind. Rees-Davies turned towards the judge:

"Would Your Lordship kindly allow me a moment: it appears that my instructing solicitor is anxious to pass me a billet-doux?" (My readers will need no instruction in the pronunciation of that term.)

"I think you may find, Mr Rees-Davies," King-Hamilton instantly rejoined, "that it's actually a Billy-don't."

Where in all the annals of that famous court can one find a neater riposte?

Before leaving Alan King-Hamilton I think it right to mention what I've always regarded as a serious wrong done to him by our Inn, the Middle Temple. Back in the 1970s, the benchers suddenly introduced an age limit with the obvious intention of thwarting Alan's expectation of shortly becoming Treasurer, an insult that grieved him for the following thirty-odd years before his eventual death as a centenarian.

❧

THE ONLY AFTER-DINNER SPEECH of my own that I crave my readers' indulgence to mention was at an annual dinner of the Administrative Law Bar Association (ALBA), held in the Long Room at Lord's Cricket Ground, as lovely a venue and, incidentally, as delicious a dinner as one could ever hope for. I recall looking out at the still sunlit square and seeing there a fox, bold as brass, taking guard (or whatever the vulpine equivalent may be). ALBA was quite my favourite specialist Bar association and I was at the time its President. Any competent after-dinner speech, it is often said (*pace* A. B. Brown!), requires not less than an hour's preparation for each minute of speaking time. My ALBA speech took fully a week to prepare. My chosen theme was that the Seven Ages of Man passage from *As You Like It* was in truth Shakespeare's thinly disguised description of a typical ALBA member's professional life cycle.

His "meuling and puking in the nurse's arms" represented his undergraduate days when drinking far too much out on dates with the local hospital nurses (there were of course no women's colleges then). Unsurprisingly after three years neglecting his studies, he went "creeping unwillingly to school" (Schools being where Oxford finals are held, the "s" carelessly omitted). The "lover, sighing like furnace… to his mistress' eyebrow" vividly describes his passionate efforts during pupillage to get his pupil-master's support for a chambers' tenancy (the reference to 'mistress' is either a mistake or, more probably, an indication of Shakespeare's remarkable prescience). The "soldier full of strange oaths… sudden and quick in quarrel, seeking the bubble reputation" describes of course the member's years of practice at the Bar, striving furiously to make his name with fearless advocacy. This was well illustrated by such as Michael Beloff and Nigel Pleming, both prominent ALBA silks present at the dinner and both, in those days, for good measure, "bearded like the pard".

In depicting "the Justice in fair round belly… full of wise saws and modern instances" Shakespeare has obviously dropped all disguise and has in mind such adornments of the Bench as (I forget which ALBA judges were attending the dinner whom I was then able to name). The "lean and slipper'd pantaloon" with "shrunk shank" naturally was Shakespeare's description of the typical Court of Appeal judge (I recall Nick Wilson – now recently retired from the Supreme Court – being there and probably therefore named him). I myself, of course, as I candidly acknowledged, was shortly to enter upon the seventh age, "second childishness and mere oblivion".

Obviously I said other things too and overall the speech appeared to have gone down well; certainly I myself recall the whole event with some satisfaction.

I am therefore emboldened to add this footnote. When, shortly before my final retirement from the Bench, I stood down from the ALBA presidency, I received from its chairman, Clive Lewis (then a prominent public law silk, now a lord Justice of Appeal), the most charming and flattering of letters. He had, he said, been asked to convey everyone's "real warmth and affection" for me and added that it had been "difficult to get the committee meeting back on track, everyone wanted to relate their favourite 'Lord Brown' moment". How I would have loved to hear what those were!

&

STILL ON THE topic of institutional dinners, I recently turned up an old email from Brenda Hale which reminded me of one such. Nick Phillips as President of the Supreme Court had arranged for one of our annual Justices' dinners to be held at the Garrick Club where several of us were members. In prospect, what could have been nicer? For weeks it was a treat in store. Brenda, however, was outraged. As the date approached, she emailed us all to say that she would no more attend such a dinner at a club refusing to admit women members than at one barring Jewish or black membership.

Unhesitatingly accepting her objection, Nick then suggested that she herself might like to find us an alternative venue. This she readily agreed to do. What she found was a new dining suite facility just opened in a previously vacant area beside Grays Inn Hall. We were to be its first hirers and there were as yet no pictures or mirrors on the walls, no flower displays, no candles or other discreet lighting, not even curtains for the windows. We duly assembled with our partners in this soulless, neon-lit space and there we dined – alas, half as well and twice as expensively as we would have at the Garrick.

The original choice had clearly been a mistake and certainly it was one for which we all paid dearly. But doubtless some (though truly I wonder just how many) will regard Brenda as having been the real heroine of the night.

CHAPTER 5

Middle Temple

F OLLOWING THE digressions of the last chapter, it is time to
pass from Oxford to the Middle Temple, the next institutional
phase of my life. In doing so, let me faithfully follow the actual
course of that transition, namely by way of student dining. It still
remains a precondition of call to the Bar (though now much
modified), not merely that one passes the requisite exams but also
that one has "eaten one's dinners". In my time we were required
to eat, during the Inn's dining terms, twelve dinners a year for
three years, thirty-six in all. This task I embarked upon as soon as
I had changed schools from history to law and been admitted as
a student member of the Inn. My eventual call would otherwise
have been delayed.

Four of us used regularly to drive up to London for the purpose.
Dining in was intended to teach one something of the lore and
customs, and indeed inculcate something of the spirit, of life
at the Bar as well as cement one's loyalty to *domus*, our Inn of
choice. We sat on wooden benches at long refectory tables in
"messes" of four, each mess self-contained both as to the food
and drink provided (a perfectly acceptable three-course dinner
with a bottle of wine), and all conversation (to speak outside one's

mess was a sanctionable breach of etiquette). Just occasionally a barrister or even a judge might join three student members and become the mess "captain", serving out one's dinner and leading the conversation. A few such dinners were fun and perhaps even instructive but thirty-six seemed excessive. Nowadays there are fewer and each is linked to an Inn event, either a lecture, a seminar, a moot, Bench Call or perhaps a musical recital.

The trick under the old system was to arrive at the Inn just in time to sign in but late enough often to find the Hall full. This counted as a dinner but of course freed one to spend the evening as one pleased: at a theatre, with friends or whatever else. Just occasionally one went to a night club, the Blue Angel then the most favoured. Just one such evening remains for me a lasting memory. That particular evening I had been driven up by a Worcester non-lawyer, Sir John Montgomery Cuninghame Bt, the possessor of a fast car and a number of fairly fast girlfriends. Having earlier in the day put two of these on notice of a possible evening out, and having witnessed my signing-in late and being set free, John decided we should all go to the Blue Angel. On then phoning to reserve a table, however, he was told:

"Terribly sorry sir, I'm afraid we're fully booked tonight."

John left it for five minutes and then rang again, this time giving his full name and title.

"Of course, Sir John," was the immediate reply. "What time will your party be arriving?"

I cannot in all honesty say that my life's ambitions were fired in that precise moment. But who knows: I was still at an impressionable age.

❧

BY 1961 I HAD COMPLETED both my Bar exams and my dinners and in February was called by the Middle Temple. In hindsight 1961 was a most propitious year to be coming to the Bar. But in truth at the time it looked pure madness. At the end of the 1950s the Bar, particularly the young Bar, was struggling to survive. There simply wasn't enough work and what there was was badly paid. Even some of the ablest young practitioners were giving up and leaving for other careers. Robin Day was just one of that outstanding generation who left the Bar for pastures new, in his case to become an iconic broadcaster and interviewer.

The effect of all this was to leave my generation comparatively thin on the ground just at the moment when, quite unexpectedly, the Bar's fortunes turned. Work began to increase: there was an explosion of matrimonial litigation and crime; economic activity generally began to expand; and there was growing intervention by public authorities in all our lives. Fees too, particularly legal aid fees, skilfully negotiated on behalf of the Bar by John Thompson QC (subsequently Thompson J., who featured extensively in my original memoir) began to increase sharply.

Fortuitously, therefore, by the 1970s much of the insecurity which my generation had so carelessly accepted was diminishing, just as it was rising for those of our university contemporaries who had cautiously opted instead for the apparent certainties of a career in commerce or industry.

We were, indeed, a lucky generation and perhaps in the event more of us prospered than really deserved to.

CHAPTER 6

Three Early Briefs

I T IS NOW over forty years since I last had a private client, since, in short, I exchanged the doubts and insecurities of general practice for the certainties attaching to appointment as Treasury Devil: an assured flow (indeed flood) of work followed five years later by guaranteed elevation to the High Court Bench.

Only when I became the Devil could I finally put behind me the constant worry of earlier years that the briefs would stop coming. Only then did I stop scouring the Chambers diary, desperate to find a future booking in my name, dismayed if instead one was crossed out as settled or, worse still, refixed so as to clash with another. In that initial phase of my practice I was prepared to travel anywhere, at any time, for whatever pittance. There were, indeed, occasions when the expenses exceeded the brief fee. But the experience, the exposure and the feeling of being wanted were everything.

Before finally parting from all such earlier cases as are not else-where mentioned, I have decided to assemble just three snapshots from those cases which refuse simply to recede anonymously into history but insist rather on reappearing whenever I cast my mind back. I shall not, probably could not, describe these cases in detail;

my sole intention is to identify the particular feature which has kept them alive in my memory.

❧

THE FIRST OF THE trilogy comes from a jury trial in which I was defending a notorious Berkshire criminal wanted by the police for questioning on a number of serious charges. As the case unfolded there came a point in the evidence when a Mercedes driven by the defendant was being chased by a police car at excessive speeds along winding roads across half the county. Cross-examined as to this, the defendant claimed not to have had the least idea he was speeding, let alone being chased: he never saw a police car following nor heard anything of the police siren sounding incessantly behind. Having at one point during the chase temporarily drawn a little way ahead, the Mercedes suddenly shot off up a private driveway and then, as the police car almost immediately sped by, instantly regained the road to drive back in the opposite direction. The police, however, had spotted the ruse and at once resumed the chase, again, on the defendant's account, without his being aware of them.

When finally the police caught up, whether because of road-works, thickening traffic or whatever else I cannot recall and matters not, my client was of course arrested. Asked in cross-examination to explain why he had suddenly veered off the roadway, only moments later to reappear and reverse direction, he said that on approaching the private driveway he had at once noticed its poor state of repair and, since he did a bit of tarmac replacement on the side, he thought he'd ask the owner if he'd like a quote for resurfacing the drive. Soon noticing, however, that the house at the end appeared unoccupied, he immediately thought better of it, realised it was getting late, and decided instead just to go home.

Not infrequently guilty defendants are reduced to risible explanations for otherwise inexplicable but plainly incriminating behaviour. But this whole story really did take the biscuit. The jury simply could not contain their mirth. Nor did they have to. I, on the other hand, acting for this defendant, had no alternative but to affect credulity: my job after all, having failed utterly to persuade him to plead guilty, was to try to persuade the jury that this admittedly unlikely story might just possibly be true. Stranger stories sometimes are. My problem, however, was that I found it no less hilarious than the jury did. Seldom if ever before can a handkerchief have been deployed so extensively to stifle the coughing and choking I hoped was convincingly obscuring my own unstoppable merriment. All too predictably, however, the trial did not end happily for my client.

&

THAT STORY, I fear, took rather longer in the telling than perhaps it justified and certainly than I had intended. Let me try to make amends with two rather briefer recollections.

First, with the tenuous link to the previous case that in this one my client was actually the Tarmac company itself. This was a well-paid brief to mitigate on its behalf before magistrates in the North East of England. Tarmac had inadvertently committed a minor public highway criminal nuisance and my task was simply to enter a plea of guilty and avoid adverse publicity.

I have said that the case was in the North East, and so it was. I accordingly took the night sleeper to Newcastle and, having breakfasted at the station buffet, repaired bright and early to the Magistrates' Court. That was not yet open so I went next door to the local police station with a view to discovering where the case was in the day's list. Being a guilty plea, I was hoping for a nice early hearing. The helpful station sergeant asked what the case was about and, on my telling him, replied that there was nothing like that there that day. Appalled that I might have got the wrong date, I got out the brief to check but no, it was the right day; I showed him.

"Wait a moment, sir," he said. "It says here: *Teesside* Magistrates' Court."

"Yes," I said, "that's this one isn't it?" There followed a brief geography lesson during which I learned the difference between the Tyne and the Tees, Newcastle and Middlesbrough, and that the latter lay forty miles to the south.

My panic must by then have been palpable and certainly the sergeant must have been the kindest man ever to have graced the police force. To cut the story short, he made a couple of phone calls, summoned up a police car and driver, had me gonged all the way to the Northumberland–Durham border where he had arranged my transfer to a Durham force car which in turn gonged me straight to the Teesside court. So it was that I arrived just before the court sat, in time to collect my wits and meet my clients.

I should perhaps add that, before leaving Newcastle police station, I had thanked the sergeant copiously for what he was doing and assured him that never before would his Chief Constable have received a letter more extravagantly grateful and commendatory than I proposed writing. Only at that point did the sergeant's patience snap as the full extent of my stupidity finally dawned upon him.

"Don't you dare!" he said. "I'm too close to retirement to want serious disciplinary proceedings brought against me now for such an obvious irregularity."

ð

THE FINAL, altogether briefer, recollection again involved a visit to a distant Magistrates' Court, this time in north Norfolk. I was instructed by Norwich solicitors to apply for bail on behalf of a local menace whose habit was to defraud elderly householders in the area by persuading them to commission entirely unnecessary building repair works.

Parliament had just weeks earlier passed the Bail Act 1976, designed to ensure that many fewer defendants continued to be remanded in custody pending their eventual trials. Such remands were thenceforth only permissible in certain narrowly specified circumstances where interim custody was plainly necessary. In our case, as I was at pains to point out, however deplorable one thought the offences charged against my client, he had here an unanswerable claim in law to be released immediately on bail.

The court took little time in roundly rejecting my application. Somewhat shocked, I began to expostulate:

"But, Your Worships, this new legislation..."

With a charming smile the elderly chairman, to all appearances the major landowner in those parts, gently interrupted me:

"The trouble is, Mr Brown, this new Bail Act just doesn't seem to have caught on around here."

There was no more to be said. My client went back to HMP Norwich, I to London. We had at least learned something of the meaning of local justice.

CHAPTER 7

A Corporation Seesaw

Personal injury cases were the bread and butter of the common law civil Bar during my early years in practice and certainly it was in these cases, both in London and on circuit, that I first came occasionally to appear before High Court judges. Judges trying the civil list on circuit, indeed, tried little else and certainly it was in this field of law that their expertise mostly lay. One such was Cantley J.

Joe Cantley, famously dubbed Mr Justice Cocklecarrot by *Private Eye* following his somewhat eccentric conduct of the Jeremy Thorpe trial, was a bluff Mancunian of the cheekie-chappie sort, sometimes stern, sometimes chuckling.

It was before Cantley J., sitting at Norwich Assizes, that I chanced to appear on one of my very first High Court cases. My client (acting through her father) was an eight-year-old girl who had had the misfortune to lose the end of her right index finger in a Norwich Corporation playground seesaw. Somehow she had caught the finger in the working parts of the structure and, as her friends began to manoeuvre it up and down, the top joint came to be severed.

I had seen the child in conference and, with the help of drawings of the seesaw, had sought to establish exactly where she had put her finger. so as to suffer this most distressing injury.

The hearing took place some months later and I opened the case in the usual way. I explained how the accident occurred and how it would have been avoided if only the local authority had properly discharged their statutory duty to guard against any risk of contact with the moving parts of this structure.

It was, alas, a lovely July day and Cantley J. was plainly yearning for a little fresh air and sunshine. After my opening, therefore, he decided that the court should forthwith adjourn for a view of the *locus in quo* (a term no longer permitted now that Latin is barred from legal use). To the outskirts of Norwich we all duly repaired, Bench and Bar all still fully bewigged and robed, the judicial limousine leading the convoy and attended as usual by police outriders. On arrival, the judge could hardly wait until, duly bowed out of the Rolls by his marshal, he climbed onto one end of the seesaw, the marshal (still top-hatted) onto the other. And up and down they both then happily went, regrettably with not a photographer or journalist in sight to capture this unusual scene.

Finally remembering that the essential object of this excursion had been so that the court might be better informed as to the exact circumstances of this unfortunate accident, the seesawing was duly brought to an end and the hearing resumed on site. My opponent (counsel for the defence) was then asked for, and on taking full instructions from his clients duly gave, explicit assurances that the seesaw was as originally installed and had never since been altered and that no other injury had ever been sustained in its use. And indeed the seesaw looked of some antiquity and bore not the least trace of any subsequent alteration. My client was then asked to show all present where precisely she had been positioned and more precisely still where exactly she had put her finger so as to get it trapped. Alas, try as she might, try indeed as all present then did to assist her in her attempt, no one was able to find any way in which such an injury could possibly result from the operation of this seesaw. The drawings shown to me previously had seemed to indicate a gap in the structure sufficient to admit a small finger. The actual device proved otherwise.

The view was thus decisive. The claim had inevitably to fail. The case was comprehensively lost.

I have never been able to work out what had actually happened at that playground. The explanation for the undoubted injury remains to this day a total mystery. The girl herself was clearly honest and truthful in all she related. So too were the two little girls who had been using the seesaw at the time. But it was no less clear that the seesaw itself was demonstrably innocent of blame.

Some years later, at dinner in the Middle Temple where I had become a fellow bencher of Joe Cantley's, I asked him if he remembered the case and what he thought the explanation might be. He clearly recalled the case. After all, it is not every day that a judge gets to share a seesaw with his marshal. As to the accident, he remained as mystified as me. The girl was unlucky, he added, that her case had been tried on such a lovely day.

I add only that Joe Cantley remains in my memory also for one other, though very different, reason. We were discussing one day the merits of the Manchester judges' lodgings (as it happened the one place on circuit my car had ever been broken into), situated insalubriously a little way out from the city, high above the old Salford racecourse. Much to my surprise, Joe said that in his young days in Manchester, the expression commonly used for *coitus interruptus* was "getting off at Salford".

CHAPTER 8

Paddington Bear

M UCH OF THIS volume I have written under the reproachful eye of Paddington Bear, now permanently resident in our Shropshire cottage and, of course, in recent years a film star.

"Is it not high time *my* story was told?" Paddington is clearly thinking. "I am, after all, a very special Paddington, brought to London by Michael Bond himself and placed in your personal custody."

"That is true," I contemplate replying, before pedantically adding, "but one cannot overlook that you actually came to King's Cross, not Paddington, and from Doncaster, not Peru!"

Michael Bond was, of course, Paddington's creator, and in creating him he created a great deal more, a whole, ever-expanding brand. Paddington was brought to me because, for whatever reason, I was the barrister chosen by Michael's solicitors to protect the brand. I do not recall ever having to go to court in its defence: stern letters threatening passing-off and trademark infringement actions invariably frightened off prospective miscreants. Which was just as well. For the truth is that I was no intellectual property expert and would have been hard-pressed to hold my own against any who were. But of course in those long-gone days, with the

Bar so much smaller, most of us were generalists; specialist practices tended to come later.

So it was that in those early years I had a wide variety of private clients. One day I would be advising on trade-mark law, the next appearing before a Divorce Commissioner, then applying in the County Court for the repossession of a commercial property, and ending the week with a criminal trial. Mention of these various kinds of case triggers many recollections, some already recounted in my original memoir; others, indeed, in the last two chapters. Here I shall confine myself to just one more of each.

&

PADDINGTON'S STORY, such as it is, I have already told. His range of goods was kept safe.

As for divorce petitions, I did indeed have a faithful firm of solicitors in Cambridge who thought me expert in family law. Divorce then was regarded as a grave matter and hedged about with inhibiting rules. If, for example, the petitioner had himself or herself committed adultery, this had to be confessed to in what was called a "discretion statement" – a sworn document seeking the court's permission nonetheless to end the marriage. On one visit to the Cambridge court, I noticed on the train journey there, within a fistful of undefended divorce petitions, a discretion statement signed by one of my client petitioners (a husband) confessing to adultery with another of my petitioners (a wife), who for her part was making no such confession. Plainly one was deceiving the court: either he was falsely boasting of a conquest or, perhaps more likely, she was being less than candid in her avowal of marital fidelity. It was not, however, for me, I persuaded myself, to investigate this question, still less to raise it with the court. Routinely I got each client to acknowledge the truth of their statements. And both petitions duly went through on the nod.

*

MY LANDLORD AND TENANT PRACTICE — mostly seeking repossession of commercial premises from defaulting lessees — came almost entirely from a small firm of solicitors inherited from Bill Macpherson when he took silk. They acted for one hugely successful property company and all their litigation was handled by a single managing clerk (nowadays known as a legal executive) called Mr André. He, I was told, was paid substantially more than either of the partners. Why was it, I wondered, that this large property company entrusted all its work to his firm? Chancing one day to meet the company's managing director (let us call him Bob), I decided to ask him. The story was this.

Many years ago, when Bob was just starting out in the property business, he fell on hard times. Unable to pay his bills, the day came when finally the bailiffs arrived. Seeing them approaching, Bob locked his door, grabbed the Yellow Pages directory, and phoned the first name appearing in the list of legal advisors. It was Mr André. Briskly explaining the situation, Bob asked what he should do.

Mr André's advice was terse and to the point: "Open the door, give them a fiver and tell them to fuck off."

"So," Bob continued, "I did, and they did, and from that time on my fortunes began to change. And I realised I would never get better legal advice than Mr André had given me that day. So I have stuck with him ever since. We give all our work to whatever firm Mr André is with."

Happily, Bob's loyalty to Mr André was mirrored by Mr André himself, first to Bill Macpherson, then to me.

ॐ

FINALLY THEN to a criminal case and it is, I fear, time to come to one of the more embarrassing cases I had for a high-profile private client. There was great excitement when Diana Dors came to Chambers with her new, much younger, third husband, Alan Lake. She by then was a celebrity, the nation's sex symbol. (This was long after the occasion when, at the outset of her budding career, about to open the village fête, still bearing her family name of Fluck, she was mistakenly introduced by the local vicar as Miss Clunt.) Lake himself was on the threshold of a successful acting career and about to sign his first really big contract with the BBC. Unfortunately he was also on bail about to stand trial on a charge of unlawful wounding. He and a well-known entertainer of the time, Leapy Lee (more elderly readers may recall his song "Little Arrows"), had spent a Saturday afternoon together in the Thames Valley drinking far too much, after which they had become involved in a pub brawl. This shamefully ended with Lee stabbing the publican in the arm.

Quite how I came to be instructed I now forget. Really I was too junior and inexperienced for such a brief. Leapy Lee by contrast was being represented by a leading criminal silk, Kenneth Jones, later to prosecute in the Kray trial. (During that trial, one of the Kray twins called Jones a "fat slob", as well as asserting that the judge, Melford Stevenson J., was biased against the defence – two comments which the judge later remarked were, together with their names, the only truths the twins uttered throughout the whole hearing.)

Besides being inexperienced, I was also absurdly over-confident and optimistic. Somehow I persuaded myself that Lake, provided he pleaded guilty and threw himself upon the mercy of the court, would probably not suffer an immediate prison sentence and so not lose his all-important BBC contract: he was, after all, an aider and abettor and had not himself used a knife. More stupidly still I came to persuade Miss Dors and Lake himself of this too. On the day of the intended trial, therefore, Lake, like Lee, pleaded guilty. But entirely understandably, as I soon came to realise, the judge was wholly unimpressed by my mitigation and showed not the slightest inclination to keep my client out of jail. Rather, Lake was sentenced to an immediate term of eighteen months, Lee to three years, both sentences later upheld on appeal.

It is difficult to suppose that any jury could have acquitted Lake even had he fought the case. And had he fought and lost he might well have received a longer sentence. But it was unforgivable to let him suppose he had a good chance of staying out of prison if he pleaded guilty, and I well recall Diana Dors, in a memoir published not long afterwards, excoriating the brash and incompetent counsel who had so unwisely persuaded Lake to take, as they saw it, this disastrous course. It was in truth a criticism to which I had no defence.

I recently tried to find the critical (in both senses) passage in Miss Dors' memoirs (of which there are several in the House of Lords library). But I was unable to locate it. If the relevant volume has indeed gone missing, I can only say that, tempting though it might have been to remove it, it was not I who did so.

CHAPTER 9

The Registrar-General of Companies

ONE CASE omitted from my original memoir among those I conducted as Treasury Devil was one I had been particularly looking forward to but which in the event rather disappointingly fizzled out. It was a judicial review challenge, most unusually brought by the Attorney General himself and brought moreover to quash the decision of no lesser a figure than the Registrar-General of Companies.

On the face of it this was a challenge which would have been expected to fall squarely within the competence and remit of the Chancery Devil, my old friend Peter Gibson at the time. Whether, however, because of squeamishness or whether perhaps he thought the issue insufficiently cerebral for his attention, Peter chose to steer the case my way.

The Registrar-General's decision under challenge was one to incorporate as a UK company a business. But not just any business: rather it was the various activities carried on by Lindi St Clair, popularly known as Miss Whiplash, the first stated purpose of her company, as set out in its Articles of Association, being to carry on the business of prostitution.

Now, by the early 1980s the UK was already a fairly liberal society, but prostitution remained, whilst not in most circumstances illegal, at least morally disapproved of. And although the incorporation of such a business would have allowed for some measure of control and indeed the taxation of its profits to the public benefit, it really could not be thought right to legitimise its activities in this overt way – it was, we asserted, clearly contrary to public policy.

The reason the hearing went short – went off at half cock as one might say – was because those advising the Registrar-General clearly felt he had no answer to the claim and, whether or not on legal advice, Miss St Clair, the proposed major shareholder in the company, had herself apparently taken the same view. Thus, when in the Divisional Court the case was called on for hearing, no one appeared to represent the respondent's side. That did not, I may say, prevent Desmond Ackner, the presiding Lord Justice, from doing what he could to inject some life into the proceedings.

Once, therefore, I had opened the case, outlining why the Attorney General had felt obliged to bring this challenge, Desmond embarked upon an an imaginative line of questioning as to what particular tax benefits might have ensued to the Exchequer from the successful conduct of this business had we not chosen to stifle it at birth by quashing its incorporation. Would there, for example, he asked suggestively, have been a turnover tax? And would Miss St Clair have been entitled to a depreciation allowance for wear and tear? But the fun and games could not decently be long maintained and all too soon I had obtained the Order I sought and the court moved on to other business. No doubt this was worthier of the judges' time, quite likely an immigration appeal. But I rather suspect that at that stage the visiting public would have started to drift away: immigration can seldom compete with sex when it comes to attracting a court audience.

In later years, Jenny and I came to know Desmond well. He was severely lame from polio as a boy but loved swimming. We had successfully recommended to him a charming little lakeside hotel at Talloires on Lake Annecy where we too regularly stayed. On such holidays we occasionally overlapped with Desmond and his wife and sometimes we swam, sometimes dined together. It was on just such occasions that, happily reminiscing about the past, Miss Whiplash's case periodically came up for reconsideration.

CHAPTER 10

Bench Call

BEFORE COMING generally to life as a High Court judge, I would just briefly mention three incidents, thus far unrecorded, occurring along the way.

In 1980, a year after becoming the Treasury Devil, I was made a bencher of the Middle Temple. In those days the Inn Bench was very small and it was rare indeed to elect a junior counsel to it. But, of course, the Devil was in a special position and I cannot pretend that this honour was entirely unexpected. Nowadays the Bench is vastly larger with several Bench Call nights a year and often as many as six or seven new benchers called on the same night, each required to speak in Hall but for no more than five minutes. Forty years ago I was the only new bencher being called and was expected to speak for at least ten minutes, the dinner in those days being held in the benchers' private rooms with some thirty present. It was an intimidating audience. I specifically recall the Lords Wilberforce, Diplock, Scarman and Salmon being there as well as several other senior judges. "A brief account of myself" was the theme required. What should I say?

I made what I still regard as my bravest, not to say riskiest, speech ever. They all, of course knew that I was being benched because, and solely because, I was the Devil. So I began by saying I was obviously well aware of why I had been elected to the Bench: plainly the Inn was recognising the great esteem my appointment had brought upon it. It was immediately obvious that my illustrious audience was, entirely predictably, much put out by this: what was this young pup up to, bragging so brazenly about his appointment as Treasury Devil?

Having thus led them intentionally up the garden path, I knew I didn't have long to bring them back down again. After, therefore, only the briefest of pauses, I said I was of course referring to my recent appointment as captain of the Middle Temple Golfing Society which, as they would all know, had that very month, after some years, won the Scrutton Cup (the annual golf match between the four Inns of Court), a victory to which I had personally greatly contributed by de-selecting myself in favour of a far more skilful young pupil. My audience at once relaxed and the event was, I believe, accounted a success.

I would just say here that being benched by one's Inn is, to my mind, the moment at which truly one becomes part of the legal establishment. At whatever stage in one's career it happens (as a junior, a silk or already a judge), from then on one enjoys altogether closer relations with one's fellow benchers than previously. Many meals and much other social life is shared and first-name terms become obligatory.

&

I RELATED IN my earlier memoir how my appointment to the High Court Bench followed on immediately from the Court of Appeal hearing in the GCHQ case. On its announcement I had, as usual on such occasions, an avalanche of congratulatory letters from well-wishers. Just one, however, has stayed in the memory, a letter from my old friend and opponent, Louis Blom-Cooper:

"Just remember," he wrote, "that whilst the office to which you are being appointed is of the very highest importance, you yourself are of none."

This salutary advice (against developing the well-known condition of "judgitis") I have since often included in congratulatory letters to other newly appointed judges, though generally with the explicit recognition that of course in their particular case there can be no need for it. Louis had plainly not thought any such disavowal of relevance appropriate in my own case.

THE THIRD AND LAST of these afterthoughts concerns my very first day's sitting as a High Court judge. In those days it was customary to mark such occasions. There would be at least one speech of welcome, friends and colleagues might attend, and the new judge would be expected to say a few modest words in gracious reply.

One such occasion (I shall not name the judge) I recall particularly. It was well attended – had his chambers, one wondered, been subject to a three-line whip or was he just more popular than we had realised? At all events, following a fulsome speech of welcome, he replied, really rather elegantly, ending by quoting that famous aphorism (attributed by F. E. Smith to Bacon in one of Smith's well-known spats with the Bench):

"A much-speaking judge is like an ill-tuned cymbal."

All well and good. But the plain fact is (and I was in the case), this new judge thereafter barely drew breath himself until the whole case was finally over.

Returning to my own first sitting day, I was well prepared. The only trouble was that no one else was. Someone, probably my new clerk, had told leading counsel for the plaintiff, though only just before he was about to open the case for the plaintiff, that this was to be my very first day as a High Court judge. But counsel scarcely knew me and had certainly had no time to prepare anything. I received therefore only the most perfunctory of greetings, far too scant to allow of anything more than the barest acknowledgement on my part. Frankly I would not have minded one whit had I known of this in advance. But to craft and then be unable to deliver one's well-honed maiden judicial vignette was, I confess, something of a disappointment, a real anticlimax. It seemed a sorry start to my new life on the Bench.

CHAPTER II

The Judges' Meeting

O N T H E F I R S T day of every term the Lord Chief Justice presides at a meeting of all the Queen's Bench judges (in my day fifty, now seventy). It is a meeting of the utmost importance. Not because of anything the Chief is likely to be saying (anything of real interest will almost certainly have long since leaked) but rather because these meetings fix the fate of each judge for the next following term. Let me explain.

Most Queen's Bench judges spend half of each term in London, half on circuit. Before these termly meetings each judge gets a list showing every circuit slot to be filled for the following term. It could be, say, Birmingham for the first half of the summer term. Or it could be Cardiff in November followed by Swansea. And so forth. It could be for a single judge. Or it could be for two or three judges. There are many possible variations. Also provided for the meeting is a list of all the judges, a rotating list which ensures fairness over time as to the order in which they get to make their choices. That basically is the position although there are various complicating factors. A few of the slots will have been filled in advance to ensure that one of each of the circuits has a presiding judge where he needs to be. Or the Chief may have decided to assign a particular judge to try a particular case (as I was assigned to Liverpool for a whole summer term to try the "welder's lung" test cases, as described elsewhere). And sometimes a Family Division judge (or even, if only rarely, a Chancery judge) would be staying at the same lodgings, though generally for just a short part of the circuit.

For the great majority of us, however, as can readily be seen, these termly choices were of huge importance, the process of selection both exciting and fraught with worry (save obviously for whoever has rotated to the bottom of the list, who has no choice at all).

In making one's choice there are many different considerations in play. What are the pros and cons of the particular lodgings where one would be living for the six or seven weeks of the visit? Are they comfortable, well appointed, warm in winter, in nice grounds etc.? How welcoming and obliging are the lodgings' staff? How good is the chef? Is it a part of the country where one wants to go? Perhaps because one has friends or family nearby whom one would enjoy entertaining; or because it would be interesting to explore it. How convenient is it for weekends at home or at one's country cottage? If a golfer, how close are the lodgings to a golf club, particularly one that gives the visiting judges the courtesy of its course? Depending on the time of year, is there some particular attraction in being there, for example Lewes in the Glyndebourne season or Manchester during the Old Trafford test?

To my mind, however, far and away the most important single consideration is whether one will be alone in lodgings or sharing and, if so, with whom. It is difficult to overstate the extent to which one's enjoyment of life on circuit is influenced by this. (If I was to be the sole judge, I almost always took a marshal, an intelligent young person at the threshold of their career, quite like one's own children except, unlike one's own children, invariably respectful.)

To share with a crusty senior judge of the old school was, I found, on the very rare occasions I experienced it, a nightmare – rather like staying with an irascible grandfather.

To share, however, with a close friend, as for example I did the Manchester lodgings with Bill Macpherson during the Arthur Scargill trial, was the greatest fun. Critically, of course, where one was on the rotating list relative to other judges whom one was anxious to avoid, would dictate how much of a risk one was taking if one selected a circuit with one or two slots still unfilled. No bridge player, sitting with the ace and queen of spades in hand, ever took greater care in finessing the king than I used to take in selecting favourable lodgings with the minimum risk of being joined there by a disagreeable colleague.

ॐ

A PARTICULARLY HAPPY circuit I remember with delight was an early summer spent at the Newcastle lodgings (a fine house with a large rhododendron garden near Durham) with Richard Rougier and Edward Cazalet, old friends, both as it happens junior to me on the Bench.

One memorable weekend they returned, by arrangement, with personal collections of private correspondence respectively from Georgette Heyer (Richard's mother) and P. G. Wodehouse (Edward's step-grandfather), collections full of literary gems. Wodehouse's letter of congratulation to Edward upon his engagement to Camilla was, as may be supposed, as scintillating and enchanting an encomium upon the pair of them, as well as upon the institution of marriage, as can ever have been written. Alas, this was not a literary festival to which I was able to contribute (though, on reflection, some of my mama's more absurd malapropisms might have induced a measure of disbelieving hilarity). I was, I may say, an indulgent senior judge, to the extent of allowing Edward to have an old friend, Tessa Baring, busy at the time with charity meetings in the area, to stay for some days in the lodgings, entered in the guest book as "the junior judge".

❧

THAT LAST SENTENCE is essentially to introduce by way of digression the contrasting story of an altogether less happy circuit which, not that many years previously, had led to Harry Fisher (son of the Archbishop of Canterbury) resigning from the High Court Bench, a great legal scandal of its day.

Fisher, a brilliant commercial silk appointed to the Bench at the comparatively early age of forty-nine, had very little appreciation of what this involved, least of all the niceties of life on circuit. This came home to him, however, on his very first circuit. Having driven some considerable distance with his wife, they arrived in the early afternoon at the lodgings they were to share with one of the senior bachelor judges (let us call him Herbert, though that was not his name). Greeting Harry's wife in the hallway shortly after their arrival, Herbert said he was delighted to meet her and expressed the hope that she could spare the time to stay for tea; he would order it specially early so she would have ample time for her journey home. Any longer stay, it was made perfectly clear, would be most unwelcome.

So it was that after tea the Fishers felt that really they had no alternative but to go their separate ways, he to his study, she (her cases never unloaded from the car) back to London. Certainly, the accepted courtesies of the day had required that Herbert's consent be sought in advance for the junior judge's wife to stay with him in the lodgings. But even had it been sought, it is by no means clear it would have been given.

At all events the upshot was that Fisher, despite having been told by the Chief, like the rest of us, that appointment to the Bench, with its automatic knighthood, was a one-way street, stuck it out for barely two years before leaving, initially for City life as a merchant banker, but later, surely more appropriately, as President of Wolfson College, Oxford. For this he was widely criticised (though personally I can't help thinking that the blame lay equally with Herbert).

❧

RETURNING, HOWEVER, to my own happier times on circuit, I shall mention only a very few more. Winchester was a prized posting with charming lodgings in the Cathedral Close. You needed to be high on the rotating list to have any chance of this. But once I managed it and was lucky enough to share the slot with Ronnie Waterhouse, a Garrick man and noted charmer. I recall Ronnie missing part of the circuit through flu and hosting in his absence a dinner party consisting largely of guests he had invited including both a duchess and a countess; Ronnie moved in aristocratic circles.

More memorably still, I recall Tom Denning, by then retired, coming as a dinner guest whilst my son, Ben, then an engaging seventeen-year-old on holiday from school, was staying in the lodgings. Touchingly, though I suspect rather tiresomely for the other guests, Tom and Ben hit it off wonderfully well and were practically inseparable throughout the evening.

Cardiff was another happy hunting ground with the enormous merit of being bang next to Radyr Golf Club, the first tee enticingly situated just below the senior judge's bedroom window. One hugely enjoyable circuit there I spent with my old friend, Scott Baker, his lovely wife, Joy, trouncing me one summer's evening on the golf course. Besides the adjacent golf course, the Cardiff lodgings had the further advantage of being within fairly easy reach of our Shropshire cottage, a bonus for summer weekends.

Those same considerations, adjacent golf and accessibility to Shropshire, favoured also the Birmingham lodgings, well sited at Edgbaston, though the accommodation itself resembled rather a chapel of rest than one of the stately Victorian villas it had obviously replaced. At Birmingham too I generally struck lucky with the judges I chose or chanced to be sharing with. It would be invidious to list them (some would inevitably be omitted), so I name just one, Oliver Popplewell, and really only because of a story which has always rather pleased me.

One day as the judge in chambers in London (dealing daily with a list of short interlocutory applications of which the judge will have had little if any notice), Oliver was suddenly confronted by his son, Andrew, acting for the applicant in a commercial case, opposed by George Leggatt, both of them young juniors in chambers together. Recognising even in those long ago days the sensitivities of some with regard to the perception of bias, Oliver began the hearing thus:

Before you open this application, Mr Popplewell, there's something I think I really ought to say. I think your clients should know that your opponent's father [Andrew Leggatt, another senior judge and a fellow bencher of Oliver's] is one of my oldest and closest friends. They may wish to consider whether to object to my hearing this case.

Can one think of a more elegant and disarming way of dealing with their relationship? I can't. And certainly it elicited no objection from either side, merely smiles. For the record, Andrew Popplewell is now in the Court of Appeal, George Leggatt in the Supreme Court.

❧

IN THE HOPE THAT this chapter may serve as a vehicle for one other judicial story I have always relished (though acknowledging that it too is unrelated to circuit life), I come to the late Barry Sheen, for some years the much loved Admiralty Judge. It is a story which Barry used to enjoy telling against himself. Towards the end of the second day of a still far from completed Admiralty Court hearing, originally estimated to last just one day, Barry testily expostulated to counsel appearing before him:

"How could you have got the time estimate so wrong?"

To which Michael Thomas QC (an erstwhile pupil of Barry's, shortly to become a most distinguished Attorney-General of Hong Kong) replied:

My Lord, we really are most apologetic. It's entirely our fault. I'm afraid that neither of us had realised how much assistance Your Lordship would be needing from the Bar on the legal principles applicable in this case.

What neater way could there be of suggesting to the judge that really in his own special field of expertise he might have been expected to have a better grasp of basic admiralty law.

❧

AS I TAKE my last leave of circuit life, a final word about lodgings. Nowadays, I am told, a manager decides on the food and drink affordable from a fixed lodgings budget. In my day things were different. We were paid a generous allowance for circuit expenses. True, some thought this a useful way of supplementing their judicial salaries. Herbert was probably amongst them. Jollier colleagues, however, were inclined rather to supplement the allowance, take full advantage of the lodgings' chef, and indulge themselves. Certainly on most of my circuits, we (or, if alone, I) entertained in some style and lived well. The many wine buffs among us (myself, I fear, not qualifying) plundered their home cellars at the weekend to bring back ever rarer and more delectable wines for the week ahead. First growth clarets as well as *foie gras*, lobster and other such luxuries were altogether more likely to be found adorning a routine weekday dinner in lodgings than served up at one's own domestic supper table. And who knows, just occasionally such circuit munificence may have tipped the balance in encouraging a wife to grant one a marital visit – not, of course, that such a consequence would have recommended itself to Herbert.

Overall, it is with rose-tinted spectacles that now, over thirty years on, I look back on circuit life with much affection and nostalgia. For every Herbert there were twenty or more delightful others. Nowadays it may well be all rather more frugal. Presumably there are fewer trumpeters and less champagne. But not all change is for the worse; I doubt there are many Herberts remaining on the rotating list.

CHAPTER 12

Murder Most Foul

NOT LONG AFTER my appointment to the Bench I was in
the queue at our local Islington fishmonger, chatting to Garry
Hart (an old friend and neighbour, fellow Garrick member, and
widely and deservedly admired as a wit, mimic and raconteur, now
alas dead). I was saying that life for me had just become rather
challenging but that, once one had got the first couple of murders
under one's belt, one began to relax. A day or two later Garry told
me I'd been overheard by someone in the queue who now supposed
me to be the local crime baron, Mr Big.

The fact is that most murder trials, although initially rather
intimidating (and I have described elsewhere my first), are
eminently forgettable. Often they are committed within the
family, usually by husbands anxious to be rid of their wives, so that
generally speaking, following the hearing, only an odd unusual
feature remains in the memory. I recall two such trials from a brief
visit to the Welsh circuit. In one the defendant was a hospital
porter who had killed his wife leaving not a trace of her body
ever to be found. Hospital incinerators, it seems, are remarkably
effective in disposing of all waste matter. The defendant in the
other case was a research Fellow of an Oxford College. Inspector

Morse's services, however, were not required: the defendant had thoughtfully set out each step of his elaborate plan (a cunning scheme to disguise the killing as a tragic accident) in a notepad carefully placed within his extensive bookshelves.

❧

FROM THE MANY murders I tried as a High Court judge, I have selected just two for brief mention here. One was a trial at the Old Bailey in the late 1980s of a man who was then the oldest recorded murderer in England. He was eighty-nine and his victim, a local schoolgirl he had enticed into his squalid flat, was just eight. It was a sorry, sordid tale. Clearly he had abused her most terribly and then, precisely why was never discovered nor in truth of any relevance, slaughtered her, using merely kitchen utensils, before finally putting her bloodied remains into a plastic bag which he deposited in a nearby dustbin.

He was defended – insofar as any defence was offered – by John Morris QC, previously a Labour minister. So inconspicuously defended, I may add, that when, at an Inn Reception during the trial, I encountered John (whom I'd not previously met but later came to know and admire) and introduced myself, his understandably offended response was:

"Of course I know you, I've been appearing before you for the last three days!"

In my embarrassment I accorded the wig more than its fair share of blame. At all events, this dreadful old man was duly convicted and it is the scene which then erupted that I can never forget. The victim's family, a large, raucous East End family who had crowded the public gallery throughput the trial, on the pronouncement of the verdict, roared out their approval, pitching forward so as actually to overhang the gallery's edge, shaking their fists towards the dock and screaming out the vilest and most bloodthirsty oaths and threats imaginable. It took some while to restore order before I could pronounce the unalterable sentence of life imprisonment (clearly in that case to be served in full).

≈

THE OTHER murder case I have selected for mention came before me on circuit in Sheffield. At the time Lord Runciman was chairing a Royal Commission on Criminal Justice and one of its members, Usha (now Baroness) Prashar, was staying with me at the judges' lodgings. The LCJ, Geoffrey Lane, had sensibly agreed with Lord Runciman to appoint a Queen's Bench judge for each member of the Royal Commission to consult informally as they wished, and I had been assigned to Usha.

The murder victim was a young woman who lived somewhat erratically alone and who regularly welcomed in for refreshment an assortment of young men, the eighteen-year-old accused being one such. She had been strangled with a hoover lead and that, frankly, was about all that was known as to the detailed circumstances of her killing. For whatever reason the Sheffield police force were convinced that this young man was indeed the killer though he had never previously been convicted of anything and had no obvious motive for the murder. True, he had visited her on the day she was killed but that was hardly enough to convict him. The suggestion was that she may have been taunting him about his sexual inadequacies or suchlike.

Put shortly, the police had interrogated the defendant for a total of some twenty-eight hours over a five-day period in the hope (and no doubt the expectation) of his eventually confessing his guilt. It was said to have been the most intensive investigation ever undertaken by the Sheffield police. But in the event he never had confessed. Certainly there could be pieced together from this long succession of interviews a patchwork of answers which could just about be regarded (at least by those predisposed to accept his guilt) as incriminating admissions. For example, having for hours denied all knowledge of how the victim died (not disclosed by the police and said by them therefore to be known only to the killer), the defendant recalled that at one point during his visit he had handled the hoover cord. But the fact is that by that stage in the series of interviews the police had themselves already introduced mention of the hoover cord and in such a way as to suggest its likely relevance to the case.

Cutting the story short, after a week's hearing spent largely poring in minute detail over these endless transcripts, and indeed listening to many of the tapes, I had become ever more doubtful of the defendant's guilt and ever surer that it could never be proved to the necessary standard. Accordingly, when finally the prosecution closed its case, I threw it out. Some would say I should have left it to the jury but I just didn't dare risk this. Was he guilty? Certainly the police continued to believe so and never sought anyone else. But, as I later learned, several of the counsel in the case, on both sides, and indeed Usha too (though she had rightly kept her views to herself during the hearing), thought probably not.

In truth the only regret I have is that I have never heard from that day to this what happened to that young defendant following his acquittal. Did he go on to enjoy an ordinary life? Did he ever fall foul of the law again? I would dearly like to know.

CHAPTER 13

Changing a Sentence

ONCE A JUDGE passes a sentence he has twenty-eight days to change it if he wishes. Seldom is this power exercised, no doubt because judges seldom have the time or indeed the inclination to reconsider decisions already, one assumes, most carefully arrived at. Only twice in my eight years on the High Court Bench did I myself alter the sentences I had originally passed. And the circumstances of these two cases could hardly have been more different.

The first, not long after my appointment to the Bench, was a most tragic case for which there could never have been an obviously right answer. Although, rather shamefully, I have forgotten all the detail, essentially it was a case of mercy-killing, by a husband of his wife, both old, she incurably and painfully ill. It cannot have been a straightforward mercy killing else, under our law, it would have been murder, just as a gangland killing or any other sort of intentional killing is murder. And all murders attract a life sentence, although of course release dates will vary widely.

In this particular case, for whatever reason, the sentence fell to me. Perhaps a merciful jury had accepted a defence of provocation so that the sentence was for manslaughter not murder. Or possibly it was a case of diminished responsibility. At all events the sentence I originally passed was one of eighteen months' imprisonment, frankly a conspicuously light sentence, even for a killing that was provoked, or mitigated by diminished responsibility. Judges are taught that all criminal killings are serious offences obviously to be discouraged, and that those committing them need to expiate their guilt and come to terms with the enormity of their wrongdoing.

As the days passed, however, the thought of this old man, locked up in a prison cell, cut off from his family and friends, grieving for a wife with whom he had lived lovingly for over half a century (true, he had killed her but only because he could no longer bear to watch her suffering), got to me and filled me with gloom. Is there, I thought, really much point in being a judge if one cannot correct an injustice such as I now felt this to be? I therefore had the case relisted before me and suspended what was left of the sentence I had earlier passed. Oddly, in terms of public acceptability, I think perhaps this was easier than had I passed a suspended sentence in the first place.

ஐ

AS ALREADY MENTIONED, the other time was in very different circumstances. Indeed it was essentially laughter, not tears, that made me reduce this second sentence. The details of this case I remember altogether more clearly. It came much later in my time on the Bench during one of my circuit visits to Sheffield. The defendant, an eighteen-year-old local lad, was pleading guilty to two counts of attempted armed robbery. The facts were basically these. On a Saturday night, in the outskirts of the city, desperate for a few drinks but with no money to pay for them, this youth had hatched his plan. On a piece of paper he wrote:

"I've got a knife in my pocket. Hand over everything in the till or I'll kill you."

This he then took along the High Street until he came to the first place he found open (the shops by then all being closed). This happened to be a small Chinese takeaway with just a single elderly Chinese gentleman at the counter. Thrusting the note at him, the defendant stood back expectantly. What he had not counted on was that this man couldn't read English and, assuming the note to be a written takeaway order for sweet and sour pork or whatever, he smilingly indicated he would take it upstairs to the kitchen. To the defendant's bewilderment this is precisely what he then did. Just moments later his irate son came storming down the stairs wielding a large metal wok with which he was clearly intent on belabouring this presumptuous youth. At this point the defendant wisely made his escape and ran off up the street.

But not far up the street because, before long, he came to a small Turkish restaurant. There, prominently displayed on the counter, sat a large doner kebab machine – a cone of lamb turning slowly on an electric spit. Noting again that there was but a single member of staff inside (in fact the Turkish owner), the defendant went in, again holding out his written demand (a duplicate copy of the one he'd had to leave behind at the Chinese takeaway).

Waiting nervously whilst the owner deciphered this document, the defendant failed to notice behind the counter the large sword-like knife conventionally used at such establishments for slicing meat off the doner kebab. This the owner suddenly seized and brandished furiously at the defendant. Who once again fled back out onto the street. Only this time straight into the arms of the local police, by then responding to the 999 call from the Chinese takeaway.

Two attempted armed robberies (even with no previous criminal record to speak of) merited at least the five-year sentence I initially passed. But at dinner that night with my fellow judges I couldn't resist telling this story and we all started laughing at its absurdity and at the sheer incompetence of this aspiring robber. And as the days passed I found myself continuing to chuckle whenever I thought of it. So I decided that really a five-year term was not necessary and that so gormless a youth was unlikely to progress into serious adult criminality. Surely he must have recognised by now that he really wasn't cut out for such a career. So I had the case relisted and found a form of words (other than that the offences had reduced the judges' lodgings to helpless laughter) to justify reducing the sentence to two years concurrent on each count. Frankly I doubt whether anyone suffered later from such leniency on my part. And it certainly saved the taxpayer quite a lot of money.

CHAPTER 14

M v Home Office

O NE UNFORGETTABLE case I tried at first instance raised the important constitutional question of whether the executive, and more particularly a government minister acting in his official capacity, can be legally accountable for disobedience to an order of the court.

M was a Zairean national refused asylum in the UK. At the twelfth hour of a dramatic day he sought to challenge his imminent removal. The detailed facts were highly complicated and confused. But basically it came to be assumed that the Home Office had breached both an initial undertaking by counsel acting for Kenneth Baker, then Home Secretary (given at 5.55 p.m.) to halt M's imminent (6.30 p.m.) flight, and also an order of the court later that same evening (at 11.20 p.m.) for M's immediate return.

Now if an individual disobeyed an order of a court he or she would normally be held in contempt of court and subject to serious sanctions such as imprisonment, fines and sequestration of assets. However, these sanctions are simply not available against a government department (which has no assets except those already belonging to the state). Civil servants in their personal capacity, and indeed the Home Secretary himself, are, of course, amenable to the court's contempt jurisdiction and subject to the usual sanctions, but only for some personal default on their part, not for actions carried out in the course of their public duties. (And I should say at this point, as ultimately the House of Lords made clear, that Mr Baker himself was not open to personal criticism.)

Not only the facts but also the legal arguments were of great complexity and the various judgments in this case, about the fate of a hapless asylum seeker, occupy no fewer than a hundred closely printed pages of the law reports. Put at its shortest, however, I held the executive to be immune from the court's contempt jurisdiction, a conclusion reached not least because I was bound to follow what was then the recent House of Lords decision in *Factortame*, holding the executive to be immune from injunctive orders (comparable coercive powers generally available to the courts).

The Court of Appeal, by a majority of two to one, whilst agreeing with me that government departments such as the Home Office are immune from the contempt jurisdiction, found Mr Baker in contempt in his personal capacity and ordered him to pay the costs of the case. This was despite his having acted throughout on legal advice.

The lead judgment in the House of Lords was given by Lord Woolf, my predecessor as Treasury Devil, Lord Templeman alone of the others adding a few words to which I shall return later. Lord Woolf's judgment, let me at once acknowledge, is a masterpiece. Much of it was directed, as it needed to be, at the ruling in *Factortame* which, it was held, had been wrongly decided: injunctions can indeed be ordered against the executive. On the central issue of whether the executive is immune from contempt proceedings, Lord Woolf reached the imaginative conclusion, for which the case now stands as authority, that a finding of contempt can be made against a government department or a minister acting in his official capacity. True, in such a case, no punishment will be available beyond an order for costs but, it was decided, in the case of the executive, penal and coercive powers as such are not required:

A finding of contempt should suffice ... It will then be for Parliament to determine what should be the consequences of that finding.

The House of Lords therefore dismissed the Crown's appeal save for substituting "the Secretary of State for the Home Department" for Mr Baker personally as the actual contemnor – on the basis that that was plainly what the Court of Appeal would have ordered had they thought it open to them and "there is an element of unfairness in the finding against him personally."

In his short concurring judgment Lord Templeman said, in a predictably widely publicised passage:

My Lords, the argument that there is no power to enforce the law by injunction or contempt proceedings against a minister in his official capacity would, if upheld, establish the proposition that the executive obey the law as a matter of grace and not as a matter of necessity, a proposition which would reverse the result of the Civil War.

I confess to having been rather stung by this dramatic – and, as I believe, somewhat tendentious – characterisation of my decision. Which perhaps explains this whole piece. But I am not, I suggest, attempting here to justify myself by rewriting my part in all this (an exercise to which no self-respecting memoirist should stoop), but rather seeking to identify the real significance of a landmark case that may once again be assuming a contemporary relevance. Had I really sought to reverse Oliver Cromwell's victory? Surely not. Even putting aside the plain fact that I was constrained in my own approach by the then binding authority of the House of Lords decision in *Factortame*, I had after all gone so far as to state in my own judgment:

The court is not abrogating a historic responsibility for the control of executive government ... Parliament assumed [when enacting the legislation under consideration in *Factortame*] that the Crown will be true to its obligations ... But if not it will be answerable to Parliament.

Was my approach therefore really so very different from Harry Woolf's? I must leave others to judge. True, the great value of Harry's solution is that an actual finding of contempt (with all the resonance that carries) can now be made against government itself. But ultimately the executive is answerable to Parliament alone for any failure. The court can declare the failure; but the court cannot itself correct or punish it. Isn't that really just what I was saying? Wasn't that, indeed, essentially what all the judges were saying at each stage of this litigation?

I add only this: Is there not perhaps a broad analogy here with the position arising under the Human Rights Act? The court can declare a statute incompatible with the Convention, but in the end must leave its correction to Parliament.

M v Home Office is, I hear, still taught in our law schools as part of constitutional law. Let the academics continue to wrestle with its complexities. I am finally done.

CHAPTER 15

Tough Hearings

W HEN MY ORIGINAL memoir was published, Mark Waller chided me for its failure to make any mention of the very first case on which we sat together, a criminal appeal in which I presided, he, newly appointed to the High Court Bench, sitting as the left winger. The thrust of the appeal was not that the appellant was innocent but rather that he had not had a fair trial, the judge having obviously taken against him from the start and sided with the prosecution throughout. Clearly I must have been somewhat impatient of counsel's argument, to my mind a rather too insistent string of contrived complaints about the judge's behaviour. We suspected also that the local (Cardiff) Bar were pursuing a concerted campaign against this particular judge and were using for the purpose a proforma notice of appeal, much to be deprecated.

When we adjourned for lunch, Mark, greatly to his credit given that this was his first ever criminal appeal, made plain his view of my testiness, observing drily that, if the appellant felt he had not had a fair hearing at the original trial, God knew what he must be thinking after my scathing treatment of his appeal that morning! I was, I recall, shamed into taking a rather less dismissive approach to what remained of the appellant's argument after lunch but it was not an appeal destined to succeed.

That recollection has prompted the thought that over the years judges at all levels have undoubtedly become less intimidating, more user-friendly. It would be altogether less appropriate these days to describe the appeal process (as one of my friends did in our early years at the Bar) as "the casting of artificial pearls before real swine".

And a story which I still somewhat shamefully enjoy and have told on occasion over the years must now be firmly anchored in its long bygone age. It is of defending counsel, mitigating passionately on behalf of a client pleading guilty to theft, reaching his peroration:

"I come therefore to urge, nay to implore, Your Lordship to show my client that self-same mead of mercy which our Lord and Saviour, Jesus Christ, extended to all mankind."

"Aye," responded the crusty old judge, "and just look where it got him," proceeding at once to pass a sentence of seven years' hard labour.

No longer are judges the frightening authoritarian figures of yesteryear. In the early 1980s, when I was appearing regularly before the Appeal Committee of the House of Lords, several of their Lordships seemed almost to vie with each other in their hostility to counsel. Sydney Templeman (widely known to the Bar as Sid Vicious) was not alone in the asperity of his interventions. Often he was matched by Kenneth Diplock, Nigel Bridge or Henry Brandon, all capable of crushing acerbity.

Desmond Ackner, a rather less austere figure whom later I got to know well on holiday in France, joked of an occasion when Nigel Bridge – plainly feeling rather guilty at his mauling of junior counsel's argument – as they adjourned for lunch, asked him, Desmond, whether he had perhaps been a little severe with the young man.

"Oh no, Nigel," Desmond says he replied, "you never actually hit him!"

And another incident which Hugh Griffiths (an ex-President of the MCC, ex-Captain also of the R & A, always a benign presence on the court) used to recount was of junior counsel, called on in the usual way in the Lords as to whether he wished to follow his leader in argument – his leader at that moment sitting down in some disarray following a sustained attack upon their entire case – replying:

"No thank you, my Lords, and certainly not without a protective helmet!"

That said, and readily accepting as I do the benefits of forensic civility in these less authoritarian times, not least in encouraging rather than inhibiting any worthwhile argument, I would add this. All the Law Lords I have mentioned were not merely immensely able, each intent above all else on reaching the right result, but their many interventions, brusque though they might have sounded, were invariably prone to cast illuminating fresh light upon whatever arguments were being advanced. Provided always that an equal acerbity was shown to both sides, as generally it was, I personally found all my many appearances before that earlier generation of Law Lords, however challenging, not merely stimulating but in truth very satisfying. A half-decent round of golf on a championship links with the wind blowing and the pins trickily placed is altogether more satisfying than merely a good score in benign weather conditions on an indifferent course. Any golfer will know exactly what I mean.

CHAPTER 16

Asylum Seekers

T HE MANY DIFFICULTIES faced by asylum seekers were an
abiding theme of public law litigation throughout my time on
the Bench. One such difficulty, of course, is making their way to
a safe country and it was this which lay at the heart of the court's
1999 decision in *Adimi*.

The problems facing refugees in their quest for asylum need little
emphasis. Prominent amongst them is the difficulty of gaining access to
a friendly shore. Escapes from persecution have long been characterised
by subterfuge and false papers.

So began my judgment in the Divisional Court there holding
genuine asylum seekers protected by the Refugee Convention
from prosecution for unlawful entry.

But the previous judgment of mine regarded particularly by
legal commentators as a turning point in asylum law was in
the 1996 Court of Appeal case of JCWI (Joint Council for the
Welfare of Immigrants), a destitution case. There, by a majority
of two to one, we struck down recent Home Office Regulations
which excluded two categories of asylum seekers from all benefits
whatever. These were all those who claimed asylum later than on

their first arrival in the UK and all who were appealing against an initial refusal of refugee status.

In a book called *The Literature of the Law* published in 1998, describing a number of landmark decisions in constitutional law over the centuries, Brian Harris KC flatteringly included two judgments of mine. One was in the Gays in the Military case (discussed in my earlier memoir). The other was this JCWI case and I am vain enough to quote here certain passages from the judgment of which I remain proud to this day. First, this, a summary of these asylum seekers' plight:

(1) They have no access whatever to funds or to benefits in kind.

(2) They have no accommodation and, being ineligible for housing benefit, no prospect of securing any.

(3) By the express terms of their leave to stay, they are invariably forbidden from seeking employment for six months and, even assuming that thereafter they apply for and obtain permission to work, their prospects of obtaining it are likely to be poor, particularly if they speak no English.

(4) They are likely to be without family, friends or contacts and thus in a position of peculiar isolation with no network of community support.

(5) Their claims take on average some 18 months to determine, on occasion as long as four years. An individual has no control over this and no means of hastening a final decision. If eventually the claim succeeds there is no provision for back payment.

(6) Quite apart from the need to keep body and soul together pending the final determination of a claim, expense is likely to be incurred in pursuing it. Applicants must attend for interviews with the Home Office and with any advisers they may have. They must have an address where they can be contacted with notices of appointments or decisions. To miss an appointment or the time for appeal is to forgo their claim.

Whilst explicitly recognising that many asylum seekers are in truth economic migrants and acknowledging the Secretary of State's right to discourage these by restricting claimants' benefits generally, I observed that failed asylum seekers now had rights of appeal and continued:

And yet these regulations for some asylum seekers at least must now be regarded as rendering these rights nugatory. Either that or the 1996 regulations contemplate for some a life so destitute that, to my mind, no civilised nation can tolerate it. So basic are the human rights here at issue, that it cannot be necessary to resort to the Convention for the Protection of Human Rights and Fundamental Freedoms [the weaker forerunner to the ECHR which had not then been incorporated into our law], to take note of their violation.

Nearly two hundred years ago Chief Justice Lord Ellenborough said: "As to there being no obligation for maintaining poor foreigners before the statutes ascertaining the different methods of acquiring settlement, the law of humanity, which is anterior to all positive laws, obliges us to afford them relief, to save them from starving."

And I ended with this:

Parliament cannot have intended a significant number of asylum seekers to be impaled on the horns of so intolerable a dilemma: the need either to abandon their claims to refugee status or alternatively to maintain them as best they can but in a state of utter destitution. Primary legislation alone could in my judgment achieve that sorry state of affairs.

In 1996 that perhaps rather florid judgment was accounted radical to the point of boldness (not a term of approbation amongst my more senior colleagues). Indeed some suggested it involved what nowadays would be labelled judicial over-reach. But the decision was not appealed and in due time the offending regulations were replaced by other provisions, marginally less draconian albeit unsurprisingly still designed to discourage asylum seekers. And one should recognise that the UK was indeed facing a huge number of such claims, stirring up widespread hostility both in the press and amongst the public at large. Judges displaying obvious sympathy to the plight of refugees were regularly the target of personal criticism. Indeed I myself was once vilified by a tabloid newspaper for deciding in one case that an asylum seeker's vulnerabilities were such as to entitle him to queue-jump the local housing list. And on another occasion I received anonymously a toy effigy of a robed judge stained by a bloody knife wound (the closest I ever got to a battle honour in the fight for refugees' justice).

The problem of destitute asylum seekers, indeed, lingered on for many further years beyond the JCWI case, next coming before me in 2006 in *Limbuela* when I was the junior member of a House of Lords appeal committee presided over by Lord Bingham. By then, of course, the Human Rights Convention was part of our domestic law and the issue now before the court was whether the level of deprivation inflicted on the applicants was so severe as to breach their article 3 right not to be subject to inhuman or degrading treatment. In holding that it was, we did not find it necessary even to refer to the JCWI case decided a decade earlier. Such is the march of time. But I like to think that overall I played a small part in developing a rather more benign approach to asylum seekers than they had once used to face and that, if and when I come to appear at the pearly gates, *JCWI* may finally stand me in good stead.

SB paintings, 1951–2, aged 14–15: "Stowe's most promising artist"
(Laurence Whistler having long since left!)

(*Right*) School hockey, spring term 1954, age 16

(*Below*) not the Bosphorus

The Islington Incompetents (playing the Gentlemen of Buckinghamshire) – Bill Keegan and his flannelled fools (SB *in dark glasses behind moustachioed Keegan, Mark Potter seated left, Roy Beaumont, standing right, not in whites*)

(*Above*) Our Georgian semi in Canonbury. First seen locked, unoccupied and for sale, on the morning we were married in May 1963. We instantly fell in love with the veranda and garden and left an offer with estate agents before departing for a ten-day honeymoon in the Western Highlands. On our return we learned we'd bought it. In 1970 we added a substantial extension and in 2008, at four times the cost of the original house, a small bathroom. Over the years the house has earned a great deal more than we have.

(*Opposite top*) Jenny's 1947 Shropshire cottage near Church Stretton with some four acres in an Area of Outstanding Natural Beauty. All that remains of the Buddicom estate, depleted over the years by marriage (Jenny's great-grandfather and father each having four wives). We took possession on Jenny's mother's death in 1987 and in 2000, to mark the millennium, added a conservatory.

(*Opposite bottom*) Chalet Brown at 6000 feet in the Lötschental (the whole valley now a World Heritage Site), built in 1977 and extended in 1988.

(*Top*) Jenny, SB and (*seated*) Ben, Abi and Dan, Switzerland, 1981

(*Below*) SB's favourite lake (refreshingly cool)

(*Top*) Our summer view: the Bietschhorn (13,000 feet) and Jenny

(*Below*) SB sharing a path in the high alps

(*Top*) Barrister, 1970s and (*below*) Queen's Bench Judge, 1984

Miniature: SB as a Court of Appeal Judge
(*painted by Jenny's cousin Dione Venables*)

Devils 1960–1992: Harry Woolf, Gordon Slynn, Nigel
Bridge, Roualeyn Cumming-Bruce, SB, John Laws

Devils and She-Devils 1975–2020: Miranda and Philip Sales,
Harry and Marguerite Woolf, SB and Jenny, James Eadie (*Louise
behind camera*), Lucy and Stephen Richards (*John Laws absent*)

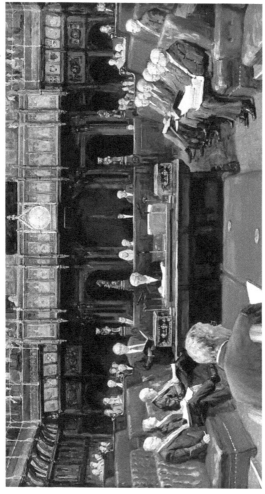

The Last Judgments of the Law Lords BY SERGEI PAVLENKO

Nick Phillips (*on woolsack*), then (*L to R*) David Neuberger, Brenda Hale, Alan Rodger, David Hope (*standing*), Brendan Keith (*clerk*), David Pannick (*bewigged behind the Bar*), Brian Kerr, Jonathan Mance, Lawrence Collins, Robert Walker, Richard Scott, SB, Lennie Hoffmann (*in row behind, by then retired*)

Harry Woolf, Derry Irvine, Murray Perahia, Nick Phillips,
SB (chairing a charity concert at the Middle Temple)

CHAPTER 17

Il Seraglio in Warsaw

G EORGE DOBRY QC died recently at the age of ninety-nine. In earlier times he had been a revered elder of the planning Bar, amongst whose protégés was a then-promising young Robert Carnwath. George had emigrated from Poland in the 1930s but retained both dual nationality and close links, particularly with the University of Warsaw where he helped found an English-speaking law school. And with that law school George over the years organised a series of seminars.

Those chosen for these visits were largely selected late at night at the Garrick, often in a state of some inebriation, and thus was generally assembled a most impressive group of participants. Certainly the time I went in the late 1990s the group included Geoffrey Howe, Gordon Slynn, Christopher Kingsland, Peter Goldsmith (each of these a peer of the realm) and Stephen Brown, Henry Brooke and Robert Carnwath (these but humble knights), a glittering collection indeed. My own selection (shortly before I too joined the Garrick) I owed to having told George that I was keen to visit an old friend, Bruce McGregor, who the previous year had set up in Warsaw a new solicitors' office for his firm, Theodore Goddard & Co. I later learned that, without so much as a mention to me, George (needing to fund the visit) had quite shamelessly written to Bruce asking, successfully, for a contribution to the costs. Besides Bruce being there, my own family roots were in Poland (the family's name until 1861, when my great-grandfather emigrated to England, having been Braun) which I had never previously visited.

What a remarkable place Warsaw is. Razed to the ground, as infamously it had been by the Nazis in their attempt to extinguish for all time Poland's cultural heritage and identity, every last original detail had thereafter been faithfully and lovingly recreated with the aid of all available contemporary records – including even Canaletto paintings. How fascinating I found it to wander the streets, not infrequently tempted into one of the innumerable shops selling the amber jewellery for which Warsaw is justly famous – a tiny violin in amber for our daughter, Abigail, being but one such purchase.

Amongst my many vivid memories of the visit, two in particular stand out. The first was a night at the opera. George for the occasion had hired a gem of an old opera house where a small opera company put on for us an enchanting production of Mozart's *Il Seraglio*. George had invited to the occasion all those who had contributed in any way to the visit and a number of others associated with the university – anyone, indeed, in any position of power and influence in Warsaw's legal life. And nearly all in our group had come to Warsaw with our wives. George was a consummate networker and the place was full.

The evening began with one of our group, David Fingleton (a member of the Garrick and the Bar, although selected for this visit rather for his distinction as an opera critic than as a lawyer) taking to the stage to introduce us to the opera we were to hear. In no more than ten minutes he gave us a most witty and scholarly account of the many different criminal offences we were about to see unfold. Truly it was a tour de force as was the performance which then followed.

My second recollection is of my own part in this three-day seminar. Mine was to be the closing slot, a keynote wind-up address, programmed for 12.15 – 1 p.m. to conclude the last session before a final celebratory lunch. It was not to be. Besides a number of characteristically discursive interventions from George himself, those preceding me on that final morning's programme all seemed intent on giving, as doubtless they saw it, very full value in their contributions. So it was that the timings slipped ever further behind and, when eventually my turn came, the clock stood already at ten to one. Now I had come a long way to give this address and in truth had worked really quite hard upon it.

What is absolutely clear is that it proved to be one of the most acclaimed contributions I made to any of the many international legal seminars I attended over the years. But, I had better add, this was only because I recognised at once that what was actually required at that stage was no more legal exegesis but, on the contrary, lunch. I therefore spent five minutes lauding all those whose contributions had so enriched our several conference sessions, said what a joy the whole Warsaw experience had been for me, and ended by proposing we all give a rousing three cheers for George. We then adjourned early, instead of late, for lunch. George himself could not have been more grateful and delighted and I clearly sensed he was not alone in that feeling. No one seemed to question whether I had properly earned my keep. And I need hardly add that most of my aborted keynote speech was later able to be recycled for use on a subsequent such occasion.

CHAPTER 18

Mob Rule

I T IS A MISTAKE to describe the activities of middle-class protesters as "mob rule". It is, at least, if one is concerned to avoid a postbag of outraged invective such as followed my Divisional Court judgment in a 1995 case about the export of live animals. Such language also tends to distract attention from the real point decided.

One can't complain about letters from thoroughly nice-sounding women who say they "don't care how high up you are in the law" but "how dare you" brand them as mobsters. Rather less measured, however, were some at the opposite end of the spectrum, such as one from a Mancunian, signing off as "Criminologist / Legal Adviser", written to Compassion in World Farming, but thoughtfully copied to me, describing me as "this totally damned, inept, incompetent, criminally-corrupt Lord Justice Simon Brown".

The central question raised by the three linked cases before us was whether the various public authorities operating air and sea ports were entitled to bar the lawful export of livestock in order to avoid the disruptive consequences of unlawful protest by animal rights campaigners. That the protest was indeed unlawful was really not in doubt or dispute.

As we readily acknowledged:

The precise point at which the right of public demonstration ends and the criminal offence of public nuisance begins may be difficult to detect but not only is all violent conduct unlawful; so too is any activity which substantially inconveniences the public at large and disrupts the rights of others to go about their lawful business.

Some of the protesters were clearly acting violently. And it was even plainer that their very object was to make life so impossibly difficult for the port authorities that they would indeed choose to bar the exporters from their lawful trade in livestock.

In these three judicial review challenges no fewer than nine parties were represented by counsel including a galaxy of the outstanding silks of the day, Christopher Kingsland, David Pannick and David Vaughan amongst them. A wide range of issues was raised over the course of the seven-day hearing, under EU law as well as under domestic law (both statute and common law). Ultimately, however, we (Oliver Popplewell was my winger) were in no doubt that the cases turned entirely on rule-of-law considerations. Having closely analysed all the leading cases in this field, we came to this critical conclusion:

One thread runs consistently throughout the case law: the recognition that public authorities must beware of surrendering to the dictates of unlawful pressure groups. The implications of such surrender for the rule of law can hardly be exaggerated. Of course, on occasion, a variation, or even a short-term suspension of services, may be justified ... But it is one thing to respond to unlawful threats, quite another to submit to them – the difference, although perhaps difficult to define, will generally be easy to recognise. Tempting though it may sometimes be for public authorities to yield too readily to threats of disruption, they must expect the courts to review any such decision with particular rigour – this is not an area where they can be permitted a wide measure of discretion.

Having refused to allow those managing Dover port and Coventry airport to decline the continuing export of live animals, we reserved our most withering criticism for the Plymouth City Council who were actually seeking a court order barring the continuing export of livestock from their own docks. Describing this challenge as "barely respectable", we said:

It is indeed a remarkable and regrettable thing that a city council are asking the court to order their own port authority in effect to surrender to mob rule.

Rereading the entire (thirty-page) judgment, those last two words are frankly the only ones I regret: it was that expression which, inevitably as I now see, the press seized upon and which so offended a whole lot of decent people, understandably troubled by the very real animal welfare concerns highlighted during the hearing.

The judgment as a whole, however, I regard as sound and salutary; indeed as having if anything yet greater relevance today than it had a quarter of a century ago. One only has to reflect on the disruption occasioned by such recent causes as Extinction Rebellion and Black Lives Matter to recognise the importance of the rule-of-law principle and the imperative need to respect the rights of others when exercising one's own rights of protest and demonstration.

If instead of stirring up middle-class resentment by referring to "mob rule" we had spoken only of "unlawful protest", the judgment would perhaps have been more widely understood and accepted. It never does to dramatise one's conclusions.

I WANT TO ADD a paragraph or two about Christopher Kingsland whom I had not come across before the Coventry case but who later became a close friend. As Sir Christopher Prout he had for many years chaired the conservative group of MEPs in Brussels. When in 1994 he lost his seat he was offered a peerage. His chambers' clerk summoned him to the phone:

"There's a geezer wants to talk to you. Calling himself Major. Shall I tell him to get lost?"

Recognising the name, answering the phone call, and accepting the offer, Christopher paid the customary visit to the College of Arms to discuss his proposed title.

"I thought Lord Prout of Kingsland," (this being the district in Shrewsbury where he lived) was his suggestion to Garter.

"By all means," responded Garter, before adding, with uncharacteristic wit: "But you do realise you'll always be known as 'the Brussels' Prout'? Why not drop the Prout and become instead simply Lord Kingsland?" So Christopher did.

In the Lords, Christopher became the shadow Lord Chancellor (to Derry Irvine) and rapidly established a reputation as a brilliant extempore debater.

Though seemingly a lifelong bachelor, he then married a most attractive and delightful Shropshire widow, Carolyn, and many an entertaining day Jenny and I spent with them in the Shropshire countryside, generally by way of a long walk followed by an even longer lunch. I continue to mourn his sad premature death.

☙

SPEAKING OF apparently lifelong bachelors, and so as to end this chapter on a less mournful note, let me take this opportunity to retell what must be one of the best lines ever spoken by a best man at an elderly bachelor's wedding. It was at Richard Hartley's wedding, only a year ago, Richard then marrying for the first time at the age of eighty-seven. His best man was Tom Shields, both of them once eminent libel silks in the same chambers, both long since retired. Remarking in the course of his speech how Richard had indeed left this step until rather late in life, Tom said:

"Many of Richard's friends over the years used to say that they'd never live to see the day he got married." (Pause.) "And indeed most of them were absolutely right!"

Alas, I was not there; it was Edward Faulks who told me the story.

CHAPTER 19

A Question Too Many

THE DEFENDANT stood charged with attempted burglary. He had been apprehended by a local policeman on the point of breaking into a large house at the end of the street. His case was that he was there entirely innocently and would otherwise have made good his escape as the policeman approached. His young barrister was cross-examining the officer:

"So, officer, you were patrolling this road?"

"Yes, sir."

"A metalled road I take it?"

"It was, sir."

"You are, I think, issued with footwear in the police force?"

"We are indeed, sir."

"Hob-nailed boots, I believe?"

"Correct, sir."

"And yours were in good condition, were they, not worn down to the soles?"

"Almost new, sir."

"And you were wearing your boots that morning?"

"Indeed I was, sir."

"Well now, officer, walking up that road in hob-nail boots that morning would have made quite a distinctive noise, would it not?"

"It would, sir."

"And the measured tread of a patrolling policeman would have been particularly obvious, would it not?"

"No doubt, sir."

So far, so good: admirably short, clear questions, each making its point. The jury was obviously attentive and impressed. But then came the question too many:

"Can you then explain, officer, why in those circumstances the defendant simply remained there with nefarious intent whilst you approached?"

"Well, sir, it could perhaps be because that morning I happened to be patrolling on my bicycle."

❧

MY GENERATION WERE all brought up on stories like that to warn us against that particular error. But advocacy training as such did not then exist. We learned what we could from our pupillage and read the biographies of the great advocates of the past: of Norman Birkett successfully destroying the reputation of the prosecution's expert metallurgist in the eyes of the jury by suddenly asking him what was the coefficient of the expansion of brass – an arcane question which he himself barely understood, let alone knew the answer to, of no possible relevance to the case and which unsurprisingly the witness was unable to answer. But such tricks are unlikely to take the young barrister far. Nor would most of us be advised to copy techniques such as that adopted by Bill Fearnley-Whittingstall QC (a celebrated Midland circuit silk) for distracting the jury's attention during his opponent's address, by painstakingly dismantling his pocket watch, before immediately then reassembling it.

Nowadays, of course, advocacy is taught, though rather to my shame I have never discovered the nature of such courses. What surely is obvious is that different skills are required depending on the different cases one is arguing: trying to sway the emotions of a criminal jury presents a very different challenge from trying to persuade a commercial court judge to accept one's analysis of some recondite legal issue. But that said, and whether the advocate's essential appeal is to the heart or to the head, I have always felt that the Bar is divided into two basic categories: those whom any tribunal wishes to send away at the end of the case with a smile on their face, and those whom the tribunal are quite happy to leave scowling with disappointment.

It is surprising how many there are in that second category. Those who simply will not stop. Those who take too many bad points. Those seemingly more intent on demonstrating their own abilities than the merits of their client's case. Those who conspicuously overstate their case or belittle the contrary argument. Those who bully the opposing witnesses or for that matter opposing counsel. And, I need hardly add, those in whom the tribunal loses trust, those they feel to be misleading them, whether on the law or the facts. It is good to be clever and articulate, but not ostentatiously, showily so, not "too clever by half", not "cursed with fluency", as one of my colleagues once neatly put it.

The majority of successful advocates are, unsurprisingly, in the first category, those in whose favour the tribunal wants to find and who tend, therefore, to win more than their share of borderline cases. What, then, particularly characterises them? Well, obviously they don't have the vices I have described as common among those whom tribunals are happy to disappoint. They needn't be particularly articulate or mellifluous: the appeal of some notable advocates (even some with speech defects) lies rather in the content of what they say: they make it really worth listening to. One prominent silk on the Northern circuit suddenly in mid-career, for reasons never clearly understood, permanently lost his voice to the point of becoming almost inaudible. But he more than compensated for this by honing the content so that every word counted.

Nor need successful advocates always be particularly clever. So long as they have good judgment and put the relevant facts and law before the court, they can generally reckon on the judge reaching the right answer. The late, much mourned, David Vaughan QC, a specialist in EU law, exemplified this. I was by no means alone in finding many of David's submissions almost impossible to follow. But somehow he used to persuade us that his cause was probably right and generally such advocates succeed on reasoning which the court itself has devised.

This too was largely the technique adopted by John Stucley, a retired naval commander with whom initially I shared a room in chambers. To deviate for a moment, John was an impressive figure and socially well connected. Periodically during his service career he had served under Mountbatten. After a while in the rank of commander, he noticed a growing number of his contemporaries being promoted captain above him. Puzzled, he got, as he put it, "a chum at the war box to have a look at the books". The last entry on his file read: "never to be promoted", signed Mountbatten. John immediately realised why: entertained ashore with the Admiral at a variety of social events, John had suggested once too often that surely it was time for the great man to tell his tiger-shooting story. It was then that John resigned from the navy and joined the Bar.

Reverting to his technique of advocacy, I witnessed it typically displayed before Claude Duveen, a maverick County Court judge who used to preside autocratically at Reading and Slough. Asked by Claude what was the authority for a particular proposition, John replied simply, "The Good Chaps Act, your honour."

Claude was delighted and readily devised for himself some serviceable legal basis for John's argument. (Invariably, of course, the most telling legal arguments are those thought out during the case by the judge himself – a really skilful advocate will sow the seed of an argument in the judge's mind and let him develop it under the impression that this compelling point is indeed his, not counsel's.)

A ready wit is, of course another winning attribute. Again before Claude Duveen, I recall Percy Harris (another ex-serviceman, a pilot decorated for bravery during the war) asserting in a road accident case that his client's behaviour had been as pure as the driven snow.

Claude testily interrupted: "I've never understood what's so pure about driven snow."

"The properly driven snow," was Percy's instant response, the balance of the case at that moment swinging decisively in his favour.

❧

I HAVE WRITTEN ELSEWHERE of Bob Alexander being the outstanding legal advocate of my generation and truly he had in abundance all the skills and attributes of the trade. He seemed also to be somehow cloaked with moral authority. Invariably he took the strength of the opposing case at its highest, patiently then explaining why nevertheless it should not prevail. Invariably he put the argument at the right level for whatever tribunal he was addressing. His style was essentially conversational and he was equally effective before a bench of lay magistrates as before the House of Lords. His towering height too was obviously no disadvantage: he had real presence in court. Just as it was always said of Bob that he never met a solicitor who did not from that moment want to send him all their work, so too it was plain that every tribunal he appeared before hoped they could find in his favour. Clone Bob and you could do away with Bar schools entirely.

꩜

I WAS GOING TO end this chapter there but, rereading it, I confess to wondering whether in truth it makes the slightest contribution to anyone's appreciation of the art of the advocate; whether, indeed, it is not a gross impertinence on my part given that professional advocacy training is nowadays routinely undertaken by all young barristers. But I have decided instead to give the chapter a new tailpiece. By pointing out that in my day, just as there was no training, pupillage apart, for barristers, so too there was none for judges either.

As noted in my original memoir, because, when appointed Treasury Devil, it became inevitable that I would be made a judge, I was required to sit as a Recorder to learn something about trying crime. That was not so, however, for all judges, particularly those appointed, as so many then were, from the commercial Bar. Robert Goff (later Lord Goff of Chieveley, the senior Law Lord) on his appointment to the Bench wandered informally down to the Old Bailey to see how things were done. The usher had to ask him kindly to move out of the dock which, he explained, was shortly going to be needed for someone else. Tony Lloyd (later Lord Lloyd of Berwick) was due immediately upon appointment to try three straight murders on circuit in Liverpool. This was the slot chosen by his predecessor at one of the judges' meetings earlier described. He thought he ought just to mention to the LCJ, Lord Widgery, that, excited at this prospect though he was, he had in fact never previously been in a criminal court. No doubt wisely, the Chief decided he had perhaps better swop places for the first half of the term with whoever was listed to sit (with the Chief himself and Melford Stevenson J.) in the Court of Criminal Appeal, a stern introduction indeed to the world of criminal justice. It nevertheless remained the case that the first jury summing-ups Robert Goff and Tony Lloyd ever heard were their own, hardly the ideal training for what is, after all, quite a serious job. There is, or course, nowadays a Judicial Studies Board and no judge today would be appointed without first having been trained for the purpose.

≈

I ADD A FOOTNOTE to this chapter, prompted by the brief reference just made to Melford Stevenson J., perhaps the last of a generation of judges entirely devoid of modern sensibilities and liable to terrorise vulnerable witnesses and young counsel alike (the proud owner of a house at Winchelsea called Truncheons). One of many stories that came to be told of Melford (I shall call him that to distinguish him from a very different judge of the same, though differently spelled, name) was of a murder case he was trying at Birmingham Assizes where the defence was one of diminished responsibility. Not unusually a whole series of psychiatrists were called as expert witnesses, both by the prosecution and the defence, all, as it happened, of black or Asian ethnicity. Until finally a white psychiatrist came into the witness box. To be greeted with evident delight by Melford:

"Doctor Livingstone, I presume."

Witty, no doubt, but deeply upsetting for the earlier witnesses and probably many others in court. One must hope that the story is only apocryphal.

CHAPTER 20

Nigel Lawson

T HIS CHAPTER spans fully sixty-five years albeit with a fifty-year hole in the middle. It begins on New Year's Eve 1954 when, aged seventeen, I was still a schoolboy, on holiday in London. Dressed in a smart new dinner jacket, I had been invited by Felix and Rosemary Salmon, cousins both of my mother and indeed of each other, to celebrate the occasion at the Trocadero Restaurant, Piccadilly, the flagship of the then great Lyons Empire, the Salmon and Gluckstein family business. We were a party of six, the others being Felix and Rosemary's daughter, Vanessa, her boyfriend, Nigel Lawson, and a charming girl, Angela Halstead, my date for the evening (whether a blind date or we had previously met I cannot recall but she was certainly delightful and attractive and one of many whom I regret losing touch with over the years).

Vanessa was, as she was to remain throughout her life, a glamorous and exotic figure, an acknowledged beauty and intellectual. Nigel, five years older than me, was plainly a rising star, a scholar of Westminster and Christ Church, confident of his great abilities and of the glittering prizes awaiting him. That said, I recall no sense of his having patronised or ignored me. Perhaps I too enjoyed (in my case a misplaced) degree of self-confidence.

Clearly I must have carried off my own modest supporting role with adequate success for the very same party was assembled afresh (Vanessa and Nigel being by this time married) for the following New Year's Eve – by when I myself was a newly commissioned National Service subaltern, temporarily stationed in Essex.

I mention these two evenings rather as the backdrop to my later encounters with Nigel, and as period pieces (are there still public restaurants with dance floors and dance bands where one might celebrate New Year's Eve? – certainly the old Troc, the inspiration for the primitive painting shown at page 87, is long gone), than to record any particular highlights of the evenings themselves.

ᓚ

FULLY SIXTY YEARS then passed before I was to meet Nigel again. All his early promise had of course by then been fully realised; the abundant successes of his careers in journalism and politics needing no recitation here. Sadly, he and Vanessa had long since been divorced but not before producing a number of highly gifted children. Vanessa herself had spent her last years living happily with the renowned philosopher, Freddie Ayer.

After 1956, bar occasional sightings of Nigel, generally in august company, at the Garrick, when neither of us showed the least signs of recognising the other, I did not encounter him again until 2012 when, finally retired from the Bench, I retook my oath in the Lords and resumed sitting there, now as a working crossbencher. From then on I would periodically find myself lunching in Nigel's vicinity at the Lords long table. He was of course a greatly respected Tory grandee and treated generally with some considerable deference. Certainly I never on those occasions considered alluding to those long ago New Year's Eves which, for all I knew, he had long since forgotten. I wondered indeed if he had the least recollection of any past association between us, even perhaps of my having been distantly related (a second cousin) to his first wife. It occurred to me quite likely not: after all, his subsequent life had been as busy and demanding as could be imagined.

In the Chamber itself, Nigel commanded the ear of the House whenever (not infrequently) he chose to express his invariably robust views on whatever might be the burning political issue of the day (climate change famously – some might suggest, infamously – being one such, literally a burning issue). Truly Nigel was an impressive orator, one of comparatively few whom other members remained in the Chamber to hear, and he took no prisoners.

I recall one occasion during question time when a newly appointed young Tory frontbencher, suddenly faced with having to answer a tricky (in both senses) opposition supplementary, hesitantly began his response, essentially buying time:

"Now that's a very good question…"

…only to be interrupted by Nigel rising abruptly from the Tory Privy Council Bench alongside, to say:

"No it isn't, it's a very stupid question!" with a witheringly curt indication of why.

It brought the House down, whether in truth defeating the thrust of the question being by then quite immaterial.

❧

IN COMMON WITH most senior Tories in the House, Nigel was a fervent Brexiteer and insistent that Parliament should without more ado implement the referendum result. For a time I, like many others, thought that the referendum had been a most inept affair, unwisely providing for a simple majority decision, posing a falsely binary question, subject to grossly misleading representations, and yet politically, if not strictly legally, binding.

At one point during the endless Brexit debates *The Times* allowed me their Thunderer column to make this case, indeed to make the wider case that referendums are always a mistake, regularly the tool of dictators, involving dangerous surrenders to the popular (generally ill-informed) views of the majority, ruthlessly ignoring minority rights and interests. I argued that we should speedily legislate to abolish them, pausing only to hold one last referendum to decide finally, now that we had learned the actual terms available for leaving the EU, whether after all we wished to do so. Though I say so myself, it was a cogently articulated piece and in the House on the day of its publication many came up to congratulate me upon it.

Nigel, however, was not amongst them. On the contrary, seeing me in a corridor, he stopped to ask whether it was really me who had written the piece. On my confirming that it was, Nigel, with his customary directness, retorted:

"Well, I hope you realise how stupid it was!"

He then produced what seemed to me then, and indeed has ever since seemed, the killer point:

"How else", he asked, "should we settle issues like Scottish independence or, indeed, as provided for under the Belfast Good Friday Agreement, the possibility of a reunited Ireland?"

To that I had no answer.

And if plebiscites to determine questions of nationhood are necessary, my Thunderer piece had clearly sought to prove too much. After all, isn't withdrawing from the EU just such a constitutional question involving considerations of nationhood and sovereignty?

Suffice it to say that it wasn't long after this that, whilst continuing to criticise the referendum actually held, I joined those who had moved decisively against the idea of a further referendum with all the chaos, delay and division that that would entail.

ॐ

I END WITH this. Nigel no longer attends the House. Advancing age and ill-health are I fear taking their toll. And now I regret never having asked him if indeed he remembers how first we met. I would really like to know. But certain it is that he will for ever remain in my mind as that older, oh so mature, so sophisticated, so clever, accomplished and assured figure that appeared all those years ago at the old Trocadero Restaurant.

CHAPTER 21

An Embarrassing Gift

I MENTIONED IN MY earlier memoir our Golden Wedding dinner for two hundred in Middle Temple Hall in 2013 and though, as I repeat, the occasion was nothing short of "magical", it has left behind one somewhat uncomfortable memory.

"No speeches" and "No presents" had been stipulated upon the invitations. Only I was allowed to breach the prohibition on speeches, our eldest grandchild, Minnie, being permitted then no more than a single sentence to propose our health. Happily, no one sought to disobey the order. And few defied either the rule against presents save, perfectly acceptably, for the odd witty trifle. But one present was to cause me immediate and immense embarrassment.

It came from two dear friends, Louis Blom-Cooper (of whom I have already written) and Andrew Hochhauser, who is here making his maiden appearance. Andrew is an esteemed senior silk, imminently to become Treasurer of the Middle Temple – and yet another friend who is not only a fellow bencher and Garrick member but also a Canonbury neighbour.

Before the dinner, Andrew had told me that he and Louis were together preparing a present that "will blow you away" (I remember the phrase distinctly). With no notion of what it could be, I naturally sought to discourage this plain breach of my embargo but was told that the die was cast. On the day before the dinner the present duly arrived, a huge box delivered by courier. And what it contained was two hundred beautifully produced booklets, with a eulogistic preface by the two of them followed by about twenty pages of citations from some of my more prominent judgments given during my time in the Supreme Court, with purple passages galore. It was clear that the irrepressibly enthusiastic Louis, and Andrew swept along on his unstoppable tide, had studiously read every word I had written during those years and painstakingly extracted every passage that could possibly be thought to embellish whatever modest juristic reputation I enjoyed.

"Blown away" I certainly was: what more thoughtful, imaginative and flattering gift could one's legal friends possibly have conjured up? Naturally I was hugely touched. But at the same time I was hugely embarrassed: the prospect of confronting each of our guests the following night at their dinner table with one of these laudatory booklets was, quite simply, unthinkable. And, of course, to my enormous discomfort and to their enormous hurt and disappointment, I had immediately to tell them so.

True, as they sought to persuade me, there had been no valedictory ceremony or retirement party or other such event to mark the previous year's ending of my long judicial career. But really, a Golden Wedding, the celebration of fifty happy years together as man and wife, was hardly the occasion for a professional encomium to just one of the two celebrants. I cannot pretend that it was just modesty that dictated the impossibility of providing our guests with these booklets. Rather it was my recognition of the shame that such a display would most surely (and, I felt, deservedly) have brought upon me as the host.

I continue to regret the hurt my refusal undoubtedly caused. And I can hardly expect Andrew (Louis alas is no more), lamenting as he must the enormous thought and effort (not to mention expense) devoted to this munificent gift, to accept too readily the judgement I took to consign it instantly to waste. But it is not a judgement that I myself have ever doubted was correct.

And so the box of booklets remains to this day deep in an attic cupboard, available for distribution to a future generation of law students if ever the time comes when some legal academic were finally to recognise the posthumous appreciation due at last to this long-forgotten judge.

CHAPTER 22

My Lords, Ladies and Gentlemen

HIGHLY UNLIKELY as it is that I shall ever be called on again to make an after-dinner speech, I am loath to leave every last story simply to vanish into oblivion. Of course, no speech should ever contain a story unrelated to whatever theme one has devised as relevant to the occasion; that surely goes without saying. But over time one accumulates bits and pieces that can be fitted in as part of a speech's scaffolding and developed appropriately to many widely different occasions. For example, I was once asked to speak at a City Livery Company's annual dinner, the clerk's letter of invitation reading:

Brevity is a quality much cherished by the Liverymen of the X Company, and four minutes or so on your part would be regarded as most generous.

Such a letter can always be woven in on subsequent occasions, if only to express the hope that one hasn't been "tiresomely over-generous tonight". Tom Bingham had, a year or two earlier, received the selfsame letter of invitation (how could one ever refuse it?) and used it repeatedly in many later speeches.

One collected too a variety of sign-offs by which to bring these speeches to an end. One such I liked and unfailingly ascribed to

Lord Denning, in his day a master of this art, was best delivered with his Hampshire burr:

I like to eat with nice people; I like to drink with nice people; and I like to go to bed [pause] with a contented heart...

followed by something like:

...and that assuredly I shall do after the most excellent dinner you have given us tonight.

Another of my favourite endings, for which I myself claim authorship, goes:

It was, I think, Groucho Marx, bidding an early goodbye to his host and hostess after dinner one night, who said: "I've had the most marvellous evening [short pause and slight stutter on the next word] b... but this wasn't it!"

followed at once by a hasty disavowal of any such feeling on the part of tonight's guests (for whom one is likely to be replying); an assurance on the contrary that for us it has indeed been a most wonderful evening.

But of course there are innumerable such bits and pieces around and really it is not for them that, highly presumptuous as I recognise this whole chapter to be, I embarked upon it. Rather I want to record just the following three stories.

&

THE FIRST I heard told many years ago by Alan King-Hamilton (previously mentioned in CHAPTER 4). It is, however, so seldom able to be made relevant that I myself have only ever managed to use it once. Let us call it:

The School Orchestra

Auditor's report to a LEA (Local Education Authority) following a school performance of Schubert's *Unfinished Symphony* :

(1) For considerable periods, two oboe players had nothing to do. This section should be withdrawn and their work spread over the whole orchestra, thus eliminating peaks of inactivity.

(2) All twelve violins were playing identical notes. This seems unnecessary duplication and the players in this section should be drastically cut.

(3) Much effort was devoted to the playing of demi-semi-quavers. This is an excessive refinement and all notes should be rounded up to the nearest semi-quaver.

(4) No useful purpose is served by repeating with the horns a passage that has just been played by the strings. If all such redundant passages were eliminated, the performance could be reduced from 50 to 20 minutes.

And if Mr Schubert had had the benefit of this advice, he would have had ample time to complete his symphony.

❧

NEXT, A STORY best told by a relatively inexperienced speaker:

The Lion's Den

Picture the scene. We are in Ancient Rome. The Colosseum. In the lion's den is a slave. The Emperor signals for the proceedings to start. A lion is uncaged and starts to make its way over to the slave, hungrily licking its lips. When it draws close, the slave suddenly bends down and whispers in its ear. At once the lion turns and slinks away out of the pit. The crowd grows restive. A second lion is let in. The same thing happens. The slave is again seen whispering in its ear. And so with the third lion. By now the Emperor's anger has turned to curiosity. He orders the slave to be brought to him.

"Slave," he says, "tell me what it is you whisper to my lions and you shall have your freedom."

"Emperor," says the slave, "it is quite straightforward. I simply tell them that after dinner they will of course be expected to make a speech."

❧

THE THIRD AND FINAL story I have often enjoyed telling (usually at annual College law dinners) and would not wish to be for ever lost, features once again the famed Midland circuit silk of yesteryear, Bill Fearnley-Whittingstall, one of whose ploys with juries I described in CHAPTER 19. Let us call the story:

A Prosecution Opening

There was a time when counsel were more theatrical, juries more susceptible to drama and emotion, than they are today. Picture the scene. Fearnley-Whittingstall is tall, patrician, imperious, a forbidding figure, wigged and gowned to represent the anonymous face of justice. The trial is at Lincoln Assizes. The charge is one of capital murder. The jury have not long been sworn in and are still shuffling around, trying to get comfortable within the narrow confines of a medieval jury box. One juror in particular, tending towards obesity, is noisily adjusting his position in the front row. Fearnley-Whittingstall rises to open the prosecution case. Turning directly to the jury, he stretches out an intimidating arm and sternly points towards them:

"If you don't keep quiet," he barks, "I'll knock your fucking block off!"

At once the court falls deathly quiet. The jury are shocked, aghast. Even the judge looks astonished. It is a moment of high drama. But it is a short-lived moment. After but the briefest of pauses, Fearnley-Whittingstall continues, now smoothly, even silkily:

"With those words, members of the jury, the accused man, George Frederick Wood, launched his savage, sustained, and ultimately fatal, attack upon his luckless victim."

What a way to grab the jury's attention!

&

REALLY, THERE'S NOT much point in going to the Bar if you haven't in later life racked up a few good stories. But alas the opportunities to tell them become ever fewer. Which is why I am reduced to telling them here. As for these three, who knows, just possibly some day some reader may benefit from telling one of them. I do hope so. That is the point of preserving them.

CHAPTER 23

Conspiracy against the Laity

"ALL professions are conspiracies against the laity." So said one of Bernard Shaw's characters in *The Doctor's Dilemma* – and certainly there is much about our legal profession calculated, if not actually designed, to confuse outsiders. Take for example the styling of judges. A High Court judge is Mr Justice X. But he's not a mister: automatically he is knighted on appointment.

I now break off for a lengthy diversion. Not long ago the excellent George Young (Lord Young of Cookham), responding to an oral question, assured the House of Lords that nowadays no honours are conferred on people merely for doing their job, however well; rather they must have contributed significantly to the public good beyond this. I later pointed out to him that it is otherwise in the case of High Court judges: they are knighted on appointment, not because of any contribution they have made outside their work, but so as to give them additional standing and authority the better to undertake it. So too presumably in the case of certain ambassadorships and other appointments. And indeed all this seems to me eminently sensible: better surely, for example, that the Lord Mayor of London is knighted, as he used to be, on taking up the office to give him added prestige when, say, promoting the City's commercial interests abroad, than, as is nowadays usual, upon his retirement.

Returning, diversion over, to judicial styling, if X J. is promoted to the Court of Appeal, he becomes Lord Justice X. But he's not a Lord (a mistake made even by many journalists and politicians at the time of Lord Justice Leveson's Inquiry into the Press). He remains a knight although he automatically becomes also a Privy Councillor, an honour which, to the regret of many in later years, our judicial ancestors chose in preference to the offered alternative of a pay rise. For simplicity's sake, I have spoken only of male judges. But of course this applies equally to women, who become dames, not knights, and Lady (not Lord) Justices of Appeal.

If further promoted, since 2009, X LJ becomes a Justice of the Supreme Court and automatically acquires the courtesy title of Lord or Lady X, though he or she does not become a member of the House of Lords. Before 2009 only male judges were ever promoted to the Lords. They then became Lords of Appeal in Ordinary, colloquially known as Law Lords. Occasionally the Law Lords would sit with other legally qualified members of the House: the Lord Chancellor of the day if he chose, or, at the Senior Law Lord's invitation, ex–Lord Chancellors, Lord Chief Justices or Masters of the Rolls. Just occasionally some other distinguished retired judge would be invited to sit, one such being Robin Cooke (Lord Cooke of Thorndon), the retired Chief Justice of New Zealand. Asked once by a non-legal colleague in the Lords what was the difference between him and a Law Lord, Robin replied: "About £100,000 a year", such indeed being roughly the difference between his daily House of Lords sitting allowance and the Law Lords' judicial salary. But of course Robin got his judicial pension too.

Reverting to judicial nomenclature, a circuit judge (junior to a High Court judge) is one permanently assigned to a particular circuit, whereas a High Court judge sitting out of London "goes on circuit". Circuit judges live at home, not in judges' lodgings: they are not woken daily by the butler drawing the curtains with a "Good morning, My Lord" before placing a cup of tea and *The Times* on the side table.

Turning next to the respective roles of the higher courts, it used to be said, not entirely flippantly:

"It is the job of a High Court judge to be quick, courteous and wrong. Which is not to say that the Court of Appeal should be slow, rude and right. For that would be to usurp the function of the House of Lords."

I have noted elsewhere that all courts nowadays are more user-friendly, altogether less acerbic, than in times past. So put the question of civility aside. Some question nevertheless remains as to the separate roles for the Court of Appeal and, now, the Supreme Court. Do we really need, some ask, a further level of appeals with all the additional expense, delay and uncertainty that this involves? That certainly was a question raised by Lord Justice Carnwath at the time the Constitutional Reform Act 2005 was radically redesigning much of our legal architecture (though his antipathy towards a final over-arching appeal body softened somewhat upon his own subsequent elevation to the Supreme Court).

For the little it may be worth, it is my own view that there should indeed be a Supreme Court, with jurisdiction, as now, over all four constituent parts of the UK (Scottish criminal, non-HRA based, appeals apart). But I add this: it should be smaller (comprising nine, not twelve, Justices); it should sit *en banc* (I can imagine few outcomes more unsatisfactory than, say, as can now occur, a 3:2 majority overturning a unanimous Court of Appeal decision upholding the first instance judge); it should (and inevitably would) hear fewer appeals than at present, essentially only those (though not necessarily of constitutional significance) raising issues of high principle; and it should cease, save perhaps in the rarest cases, hearing Privy Council appeals – these should rather be heard by Court of Appeal judges, all qualified to sit in the Judicial Committee of the Privy Council as already explained.

The fundamental changes brought about in our legal structures by the Constitutional Reform Act included, most unfortunately as I believe, the dismemberment of the historic office of Lord Chancellor, stripping him of his role as head of, and appointer of, the judiciary, and of his Speakership of the House of Lords. This much diminished figure is now but a shadow of Lord Chancellors past. The holder of the office used to be of the highest standing and wield great influence: an authoritative figure at the zenith of his own political career and with no axe left to grind; at the heart of government, indeed the very conscience of government, there to safeguard the enduring values of the rule of law and the independence of the judiciary.

Nowadays, the Lord Chancellor, doubling up as Secretary of State for Justice, inappropriately responsible for both the administration of criminal justice and the prison estate, is a career politician, often comparatively junior and with continuing personal political ambitions, sometimes with no legal background whatever, and, as amply demonstrated by the "Enemies of the People" case (the *Daily Mail's* ill-judged headline following the Divisional Court's judgment in *Miller 1* requiring parliamentary agreement to the UK giving notice to withdraw from the EU), on occasion careless of the Lord Chancellor's express statutory responsibility for defending the rule of law. In the last ten years no fewer than six different ministers have held this much depleted office, not all with conspicuous success, some indication surely of the low esteem in which it is now held and certainly not conducive to its most effective discharge.

By the 2005 Act, the Lord Chancellor also lost his power of patronage. A new Judicial Appointments Commission replaced the "tap on the shoulder" by which outstanding young silks once used to be persuaded, at some personal sacrifice, to accept early appointment to the Bench.

All these and certain other lesser changes can of course be defended as advancing the interests of transparency, perception and the separation of powers. Some indeed argue that they had become essential to our continued compliance with the ECHR. That I respectfully question. But much of my lingering regret at these changes will, I recognise, be ascribed by many rather to the nostalgia of advancing age than to any intrinsic advantage in the old arrangements. My case would rest principally upon the deeply regrettable dismantling of the Lord Chancellorship. Though I would admit also to some sympathy with Lord Campbell's historic expostulation at an earlier proposed reform:

"Reform, reform. Good God man, aren't things bad enough as they are already?"

❧

I WANT TO CONCLUDE this ragbag chapter of disparate legal reflections by reference to an essay on "Dissenting Judgments" that I wrote some years ago for an OUP publication to commemorate Alan Rodger (*Judge and Jurist – Essays in Memory of Lord Rodger of Earlsferry*). I am prompted to do so because of its possible relevance to the recent unanimous decision of the eleven justices of the Supreme Court in *Miller 2*, the prorogation case.

The essay as a whole discusses in some detail the pros and cons of dissents in a variety of contexts including of course final appellate courts, and at one point I note that it was once said (by either Lord Wilberforce or Lord Ackner) that a member of the appellate committee of the House of Lords "dissents only when his exasperation at the sheer stupidity of his colleagues outweighs his own natural indolence."

More relevant for present purposes, however, is this passage, which follows on from my recognition that in the great majority of final appeals a dissent will have no sensible prospect of ever influencing the future development of the law:

Does that, however, mean that a dissent in such circumstances would constitute, as some would say, no more than a futile gesture and that it should therefore be discouraged? I would suggest not. On the contrary, there are many occasions when, as I would contend, however plain it may be that a dissent will no more influence the future development of the law than the outcome of the particular appeal before the court, a judge should nevertheless, assuming always that he or she is clear in his or her own mind that the majority's view is wrong, give a reasoned judgment saying so.

In the administration of justice, it has been said, the most important single person in court is the defeated litigant. Generally, the terms of the majority judgment or judgments will make it plain that the losing party's arguments have been fully heard and taken into account and will explain why they have nevertheless not prevailed. But that is not invariably so. And whether or not that is so, it seems to me that nothing is better calculated than a dissenting judgment to demonstrate beyond question that the losing side's case has been properly understood and, indeed, recognized to have real force, force sufficient to persuade one member of the court at least that it was right. This may be of comparatively small comfort. Some might suggest even that it may compound the litigant's disappointment to think that he or she came so close to success. In my experience, however, the losing party greatly prefers to realize that the strength of his argument was properly recognized than to be left wondering if his case was ever really put across to the court. And, although no doubt this matters less, that is true of the defeated litigant's lawyers no less than of the litigant himself. If, moreover, any of the judges below (whether at first instance or in the Court of Appeal) happened to differ in their conclusion from that arrived at by the majority in the Supreme Court, they too may be expected to feel gratified and to a degree reassured by a dissent which indicates that their views were not perhaps after all so plainly erroneous.

Now all this, of course, is directly relevant only in a case where one at least of the judges is of the clear view that the majority is mistaken. Turning then to *Miller 2*, it appears that no one was. This I regret. But what more particularly I regret is that the unanimous Supreme Court judgment stands in the sharpest and largely unexplained distinction to the unanimous first instance decision of a most authoritative Divisional Court consisting of the Lord Chief Justice, the Master of the Rolls and the President of the Queen's Bench Division. I do not say that the Supreme Court decision is wrong; on the contrary, I believe that it can and must be justified on the narrow factual basis that, at that stage, the government, for whatever reason, refused to put forward any but the most obviously unsustainable justification for so long a prorogation, namely the need to write a Queen's Speech. The Divisional Court by contrast had recognised that there were additional underlying political reasons for the prorogation, reasons beyond the court's proper competence to judge.

Given the obvious constitutional importance and sensitivity of the case, given the wide public expectation that the courts would be unlikely to interfere with the parliamentary process, and given the apparent strength and authority of the Divisional Court's own reasoned judgment and ruling, surely the very least that was required of the Supreme Court was a full explanation of why and where the first instance judges were to be regarded as so profoundly mistaken in their judgment. I recognise of course the pressures of time the Supreme Court was under, but if I were one of the Divisional Court judges, I would feel distinctly bruised by all this.

Frankly, I would have preferred at least one dissent. For the reasons given in the passage in my essay quoted above, I believe that would have strengthened, not weakened, the judgment as a whole (as in my view the Supreme Court's decision in *Miller 1* was actually strengthened by the three dissents). But above all I believe that it would have gone some way to allay the feeling, indeed the conviction, of many Brexiteers and others who so strongly supported the government on this issue, that this was in fact a stitch-up, with a predetermined outcome, unanimity agreed under pressure in advance. In short, ending this chapter with an echo of its opening note, I worry that too many (and not least amongst them a number of influential Tory politicians) regard the Justices here as having conspired against the laity. Of course I know full well that they did no such thing – the very idea is absurd and outrageous. But where perception is of such importance, sadly *Miller 2* leaves many uneasy.

❧

AS A POSTSCRIPT I should note that some passages from this piece have already appeared with my permission in *Prospect*.

CHAPTER 24

Opening Lines

MY VERY LAST sitting before retirement was as a member of the judicial committee of the Privy Council in Mauritius for the last week of March, 2012, five long court days with packed lists. The visit, though most excellently led by David Hope, was exhausting, socially as well as forensically. We then flew back overnight to Gatwick, arriving early on the Saturday morning.

Through a combination of my as yet undiagnosed bowel cancer and regret at finally reaching retirement, I was already feeling pretty low when we boarded the plane. On the flight back David and I had adjacent sleeping-pods and, recognising I needed cheering up, he lowered the dividing partition between us and we chatted throughout much of the night. Having flattered me upon my contribution to the trip (and, indeed, to the court as a whole over our many years sitting together), charmingly and self-deprecatingly David told me the story of his own unexpectedly swift progression. His meteoric rise really began with his election by the narrowest of margins to Dean of the Faculty (leader of the Scottish Bar). This was followed by appointment direct to Lord President (Scotland's most senior judge) and then long years as a Law Lord, before finally becoming Deputy President of the new Supreme Court. It was a remarkable career for someone so genuinely modest and unassuming.

Reverting to our return journey, the long night over, we duly arrived at Gatwick around 6.30 in the morning, each of us to be met by an Addison Lee driver contracted to the Government Car Service. Speedily the Lords Hope, Mance, Dyson and Sumption bade their successive farewells and were in turn driven away. Soon, I alone was left. To cut this gloomy story short, with growing impatience and irritation, feeling like death, I waited a while and then embarked on a series of ever more frustrating phone calls.

In the event it was not until nine o'clock that my driver at last arrived, only then, as I later learned, having finally been awakened by Addison Lee from his deep slumber in the Gatwick carpark. The journey home, the traffic by then much thicker than had we started on time, was punctuated by the driver's repeated pleas for me not to make a complaint which would most certainly cost him his job. Of course I didn't: inertia is a powerful force. And besides, the likely explanation for his carpark nap was his being worked too hard. One hopes, however, that not too many of his later fares suffered similarly: it had been a dispiriting experience, a sorry end to my final week's sitting.

It was not, however, quite the end of my judicial life. I still had to write the two reserved judgments which David had assigned to me during the visit. One of these I wrote quickly with no difficulty. The other, conscious that it was to be my very last judgment, occupied me for much of the time between my cancer diagnosis on the Monday after our return and my admission to the London Clinic a fortnight later.

Having thought long and hard about the opening line (the central topic of this chapter), I finally decided on:

Is there a mango tree in the respondent's backyard at No. 303 Nelson Mandela Avenue, Quatre Bornes?

This, I felt – though hardly matching Denning's celebrated: "It was bluebell time in Kent" – was an arresting enough start, giving the judgment the distinctively tropical (if not specifically Mauritian) flavour it needed. It was, moreover, a relevant introduction to the essential problem thrown up by the case: the lamentable practice of even the higher courts in Mauritius (in common regrettably with those of many other post-colonial jurisdictions) of treating litigation as an endless procedural game, repeatedly postponing the court's central task of actually deciding the case. Almost always the final decision is likely to turn on the underlying factual disputes between the parties. It is these, therefore, that the courts should be striving to resolve.

This particular case had begun marginally over ten years earlier. During that time it had been litigated repeatedly up and down the Mauritian court hierarchy, on a whole succession of nit-picking, technical, procedural points, always leaving the basic factual issues not merely unresolved but entirely unaddressed. One such issue concerned the mango tree – quite how and why, I have now forgotten and matters not. It should long since have been decided and I felt amply justified in describing the line of legal authority invoked to explain these endless delays in the process as:

a blot on Mauritius's generally estimable record for the fair administration of justice … [a blot which] must not be allowed to continue.

꙳

NO ESSAY touching on the opening lines of judgments could excusably omit the beginning of Denning's renowned dissenting judgment in *Miller v Jackson*, a 1977 nuisance case:

In summertime village cricket is the delight of everyone. Nearly every village has its own cricket field where the old men play and the young men watch. [And so it had been in that particular village for the last seventy-five years.]

As I need hardly observe, that was not a promising start for the incoming homeowner trying to protect such of his windows as faced the village green.

To those interested in Denning's judgment styles I cannot sufficiently recommend Sir Martin Nourse's Denning Society lecture given on this topic some years ago. It is a masterly analysis of a fascinating subject.

❧

IT WOULD REQUIRE a degree of forbearance way beyond any at my command to refrain at this point from quoting a generous recent review of my memoir, *Playing off the Roof*, in the *Middle Templar*, the Inn's Yearbook, a review contributed by my old friend and Court of Appeal colleague, Andrew Longmore. The passage I am altogether too vain to resist quoting refers to a seminar on judgment writing given for the higher judiciary some years ago by Tom Bingham. Andrew writes:

He [Tom] began by saying that the opening paragraph of any judgment of [Lord] Brown was invariably a model of how a judgment should begin. He then read a couple of examples and it was apparent that they contained a succinct summary of the issues in the case which anyone could understand.

What greater praise could one receive than to be cited as an exemplar by Tom Bingham, himself the acknowledged master of the art? This is a tribute to be treasured. I recognise, of course, the immodesty of this closing section. But I care not. It is a price worth paying for the chance now to savour, cherish and actually broadcast this accolade.

❧

The Hope Diaries

THE ABOVE REFERENCE to David Hope requires, I think, some comment on an issue that has proved somewhat contentious in legal circles.

Over the years, David has published a series of diaries from the successive stages of his professional life. These, particularly the later volumes recording his time as a serving judge, have been sharply criticised within the profession, not least by several of those with whom he sat in the various appeal courts. For my part, however, I take a rather less critical view. True, they provide unusually candid character descriptions and accounts of how certain judicial decisions were arrived at. And perhaps on occasion these border on the indiscreet. Some, certainly, will think this unwise. But it seems to me excessively harsh to suggest that these entries involve the betrayal of confidential exchanges. Could they not rather be regarded as a useful historical record of David's life and times? He was, after all, prominent in other areas of Scottish life besides the law.

I should perhaps add, however, that, in contrast to one or two others, such references as the diaries make to me are unfailingly generous.

CHAPTER 25

Stone the Crows

ALTHOUGH GOLF LOOMED fairy large in my original memoir I had not proposed to serve up any second helpings of this particular course (allow me the pun). I had rather supposed that after some seventy-five years at the game there would be little new to add. And so it seemed until, this further volume all but complete, playing one last round at Church Stretton before returning south after our long Covid-prompted exile in Shropshire, I encountered what was for me a brand new golfing experience.

As mentioned in the earlier volume, Church Stretton Golf Club is the second highest in the land with spectacular views over several counties. And, indeed, as I recently learned, it also now boasts golf.com's accolade of being one of the twenty-five best sub-6000-yard golf courses in the entire world, a judgement I have no difficulty in accepting. Situated on high moorland above the town, it is grazed by large numbers of mountain sheep and a few wild horses too (the greens being altogether too well tended and close-mown to be of the slightest interest to any of these).

Now to my novel recent golfing experience. No, I didn't hit and stun, let alone kill, a horse or even a sheep. All I did, and this of course was very far from a novel experience, was to duff my drive on the seventeenth, hitting it a mere fifty yards up the fairway. At which point a huge black crow flew noisily across the fairway, swooped down, took the ball instantly into its beak and, utterly ignoring my despairing shouts, carried it across the rough, over the boundary fence.

"Out of bounds," cried (or do I mean crowed?) my playing partners as the crow proceeded down the steep hillside to goodness knows where, in the wilderness beyond, its expectant family were no doubt hungrily awaiting their next meal. I have suffered in the past from the occasional displacement of my golfball by an errant dog or child. But never before have I had my ball mistaken for an egg and so shamelessly taken away.

Or had that crow, I began to wonder, seen me drive and decided the time had come when I needed somehow to be discouraged from continuing my ever less convincing efforts to play the game? Was it, indeed, not so much carrying my ball away as carrying a subtle message to me? As my mobility decreases and buggies have become ever more a necessity, that crow has given me, I confess, pause for thought.

CHAPTER 26

Trial by Jury

THIS CHAPTER CONSISTS essentially of a lecture I gave at Oxford in 2010 entitled "Are Juries a Good Thing? The Jury is Out". It was the High Sheriff's annual lecture given to a large, mixed-ability audience, ranging from A-level schoolchildren to law dons, in the cavernous Oxford Schools building in the High, on the pros and cons of trial by jury.

Originally I had planned simply to include the lecture as an annex at the end of the book (just as the Strasbourg lecture I gave in 2012 was annexed to my earlier memoir). But I decided instead to make it the subject of a separate chapter when I came to recognise that the right to jury trial is again now a highly topical issue, and became anxious to make the point that there is really nothing particularly revolutionary, no slaughtering of sacred cows, involved in the proposal many of us are currently advancing, namely for more trials by judge alone. The plain fact is that the criminal justice system is currently in crisis, realistically a crisis that only some attenuation of the present requirement for jury trial can hope to resolve.

At the start of the Covid pandemic there was already a most regrettable backlog of some 37,000 criminal cases awaiting jury trial. Following the lockdown, that backlog has grown inexorably and, hardly surprisingly, despite everyone's best efforts to overcome the continuing logistical challenges, it shows no signs of abating. The only legislative response thus far has been by way of regulations to extend custody time limits so that prisoners awaiting trial can be detained for even longer before their guilt or innocence is established. Should they not be allowed instead to choose to be tried by judge alone (or perhaps a judge sitting with two magistrates, as currently hear appeals from the Magistrates' Court)? At present, not even the defendant can ask to be tried by judge alone. Must victims and witnesses be required to wait ever longer, their nerves stretched, their memories fading, their evidence consequently weakening, before they can draw a line under this most nightmarish period of their lives, and can at last see justice done?

As those who now read this lecture will see, the present right to jury trial really owes nothing to Magna Carta (a shibboleth promoted by a few diehard civil libertarians), has evolved gradually and been repeatedly modified over the years, and has never anyway been an absolute right. Exceptions exist for Irish terrorist cases (the Diplock courts, still operating), cases of jury tampering and, most importantly, cases that at any given time are regarded as falling at the lower end of the scale of criminal seriousness (for example the theft of goods below a certain value).

For the reasons set out in the lecture which now follows, I remain overall a supporter of trial by jury. But I see no reason why it should for all purposes and in all circumstances be regarded as inviolate, to the point where it necessarily outweighs all possible countervailing considerations. Of course any change would require primary legislation. But surely there can be few more compelling claims for space in the currently crowded legislative programme than the urgent need to bring our criminal justice system back into workable order. That at any rate is my view.

The text of the lecture now follows. I should just say that its opening story of Robert Maxwell's libel action against *Private Eye* will be familiar to anyone who has read my original memoir where it occupied a chapter of its own. But I have thought it right nevertheless to publish the lecture as delivered and so the story reappears here.

꙾

The High Sheriff's Law Lecture
12 October 2010, OXFORD

"Are Juries A Good Thing? The Jury Is Out"

THIS IS FAR too large and daunting a gathering to attempt anything other than to read this lecture. But at the same time, with a captive audience, I cannot resist the opportunity of beginning with just one story from my own experience of juries. It dates back, I fear, nearly a quarter of a century. And it concerns a civil case in the Royal Courts of Justice, whereas this lecture deals almost exclusively with juries in criminal cases.

The case was *Maxwell v Private Eye*, a high profile case of its time. The late Robert Maxwell, then a resident of this great city, although perhaps not its proudest son, was suing *Private Eye* for libel. The essence of his case was that the *Eye* had published an article about his relationship with Neil Kinnock, then the leader of the Labour Party, insinuating that he, Maxwell, had been trying to bribe Kinnock with gifts of free travel and the like into recommending him for a peerage. *Plus ça change*.

Like all jury trials the case was proceeding at a leisurely pace when on the fourth day I returned from lunch in my Inn, the Middle Temple, to find a note from the jury awaiting me. It was a brief note and it read quite simply:

"Please Sir, can you tell us what a peerage *is?*"

So there it was, already three and a half days spent on a libel trial where the central issue for the jury was whether the article complained of contained an innuendo that Maxwell had been corruptly trying to get Neil Kinnock to recommend him for a peerage and the jury still didn't understand what it was that was actually being alleged. Obviously I then had to explain what is meant by a peerage and basically what the House of Lords does and so forth and on we went. The next day at lunch I couldn't resist telling my fellow benchers what had happened and adding:

"Isn't that an astonishing thing – not a single member of the jury knew what a peerage is?"

To which one of my fellow benchers, a rather dry chancery silk, replied:

"No, that doesn't necessarily follow. One of them might have known and explained it to the others and been flatly disbelieved!"

I learned two lessons from that case: first, that jurors aren't always terribly smart; secondly, that peerages aren't all that they are cracked up to be. Most people don't know what they are, and those that do nowadays seem intent on abolishing them anyway.

TO MY TASK: are juries a good idea?

Barely a week goes by without some discussion of the merits or demerits of jury trial. Only yesterday, in the Middle Temple, there was a debate on the motion "Trial by jury ever has been and I trust ever will be looked upon as the glory of the English law". Lord Justice Hooper agreed with that; Professor Cheryl Thomas of UCL – who earlier this year published a report based on empirical research entitled *Are Juries Fair?* – was less sure. Down the years, many have acclaimed the jury system, often in terms of extravagant hyperbole; many have criticised it, often with equal trenchancy.

Blackstone in the 18th century described it as "the glory of the English law; the benchmark of liberty; the palladium of justice". Sir Patrick Devlin (later Lord Devlin), in his Hamlyn lectures half a century ago, famously called it "the lamp that shows that freedom lives". An American academic, writing in 1937, put it rather differently:

We commonly strive to assemble 12 persons colossally ignorant of all practical matters, fill their vacuous heads with law they cannot comprehend, obfuscate their several intellects with testimony which they are incompetent to analyse or unable to remember, permit partisan lawyers to bewilder them with their meaningless sophistry, then lock them up until the most obstinate of their number coerce the others into submission or drive them into open revolt.

And one may recall Hilaire Belloc, rather more pithily if no less cynically, describing a jury as twelve people summoned at random to decide who has the better lawyer.

Before turning to unpack some of the rhetoric and to examine some of the real advantages and disadvantages of jury trial, it is worth glancing at its history and recognising that as an institution it has changed vastly down the centuries, not least in recent times.

Many of those most passionately opposed to any encroachment upon the use of juries not only ignore this history and the gradual evolution of the jury system but firmly ascribe its origins to Magna Carta 1215, a supposed derivation which, of course, gives their case terrific resonance and apparent irrefutability.

As Tony Hancock, a comedian whom the older amongst us will recall, remarked in his version of the famous Henry Fonda film, *Twelve Angry Men*: "Think of your roots, think of your history. Magna Carta, did she die in vain?"

(*Twelve Angry Men*, I may add parenthetically, is a menace to the criminal justice system. Whenever, some years back, sitting as a High Court judge with a jury at the Old Bailey or some Crown Court around the country I was trying serious crime and the film was shown on TV, I used to find that it was immediately followed by a rash of perverse acquittals.)

But back to Magna Carta 1215. Until that time the usual way of deciding criminal cases was trial by ordeal, the ordeal, that is, of fire or water, or trial by battle. As it happens, in the very same year as Magna Carta, the Lateran Council ended trial by ordeal and this caused real problems because the alternative, trial by battle, was not available in a number of cases, particularly for women.

Thus it was that increasingly cases began to be decided by reference actually to the evidence – i.e. by reference to the facts of the case and the likelihood of the accused having actually committed the offence as opposed to whether he could win in battle, or survive ordeal by fire or water. And this is where jurors came in. Any legal historians present will recognise all this as a huge over-simplification of the position – there are, of course, many lengthy and erudite tomes on the history of the jury system.

But for present purposes I make just two points.

First, that these early jurors were not remotely like the jurors of today. They were twelve men from the neighbourhood who had personal knowledge of local affairs, not least of the defendant's reputation in the neighbourhood. In short, they swore to the truth of what they knew. So far from deciding the case upon the evidence brought before them, they actually *gave* the evidence. Today, they would be automatically disqualified from acting as jurors at all – the very point of jurors nowadays being, of course, that they know nothing whatever about the facts of the case and therefore bring a wholly unprejudiced mind to bear upon the evidence given by the various witnesses.

Secondly, do not be misled by that oft-cited provision in Magna Carta (and I abbreviate):

No free man shall be imprisoned except by the lawful judgment of his peers.

The reference there to "free men" excluded the villeins (spelt with an "e") and indeed excluded most ordinary people. The essence of Magna Carta has been aptly summarised as "one baron, one vote". It did little to secure justice for the common man.

MOVING ON, quite apart from the jury's basic change from a body of witnesses to a fact-finding tribunal, the nature of juries, and jury trials, as I observed earlier, has changed down the years. About the only thing that hasn't changed is the number of jurors constituting the jury – twelve for a criminal trial in England and Wales, although in Scotland fifteen, and for a coroner's jury only seven. And, indeed, even in England, since 1965 a criminal trial can continue with as few as nine members if up to three have died or for any reason been discharged. The fact is that virtually everything about juries save only the number who are sworn in at the start of the trial has changed and indeed changed repeatedly.

Who gets called for jury service? Once it was twelve good men and true. Well, whether invariably good and true may be doubted, but certainly it was men only until after the First World War when, in 1919, women were first admitted for jury service. But not many women: until the 1970s only property owners or householders were eligible to serve and inevitably most of those were men. Until the 1970s, moreover, the age range was only 21 – 60. It was then increased to 18 – 70, this upper limit now once again being under active reconsideration with a view to its further extension to 75, 80 or possibly even without limit.

In addition, just as these basic qualifications for jury service – property rights and age limits – were being enlarged during recent times, so too most of the categories of ineligibility were being swept away. Until recently, more or less anyone who had anything to do with the law was ineligible: judges and JPs, solicitors and barristers, court staff, prison officers, probation officers, members of police authorities – in short, very many of those here today.

Not so now, however. In 2004 even judges became eligible for jury service and one of the first of these, then a member of the Court of Appeal, now a colleague of mine in the Supreme Court, was called for jury service, oddly enough in the very same building where the Supreme Court now sits. He entertainingly recalls his own experiences as a juror, although, since section 8 of the Contempt of Court Act 1981 forbids any disclosure of what goes on in the jury room, only one is repeatable.

That was a fellow juror's reaction to when my colleague, about to be empanelled for a particular trial, was waved aside by the judge, an old friend of his, with the words:

"Oh dear. I'm afraid I know this juror far too well for him to be sworn in this case."

"Cor," said his fellow juror, "what you been up to then? It must have been something pretty terrible for the judge to remember you!"

UNDOUBTEDLY, THEREFORE, there has been a move in recent times towards a wider pool of jurors. And other changes too have been made with a view to achieving something like a cross-section of society in jury selection. The defence used to be allowed seven peremptory challenges. They could in other words object to up to seven jurors without giving any reason at all – although very often this seemed to be because the juror was wearing a jacket and tie or carrying a copy of the *Daily Telegraph*. And if there were several defendants, each had seven challenges so that collectively they could more or less shape a jury to their choice.

In 1977, however, the number of peremptory challenges was reduced from seven to three and in 1988 it was abolished altogether. But it would be wrong to suppose that the result of all these changes has in fact been to ensure a good cross-section of the population in every case. Far from it. As the years have passed, criminal trials have taken longer and longer and the result has been, at least in many of the more serious cases, juries for the most part composed of the elderly and the unemployed. Those in work are generally excused from long cases.

At the Old Bailey 250 years ago, sixty-two cases were heard in just five days. Nowadays a jury trial can last for many months, sometimes indeed for over a year. Investigations are more thorough. Police interviews are longer. Scientific evidence of every kind has proliferated with ever newer techniques of investigation and proof. Computer evidence is now commonplace. So too, logs of phone calls, evidence which maps the use of cell phones, endless fax and email communications, and, of course, the ever energetic photocopier.

AMONGST THE MANY other changes made down the years to the process of jury trial let me briefly mention just two.

First, the abolition of the unanimity principle which had applied for centuries and was still being steadfastly supported by Lord Devlin in his 1956 lectures. Majority verdicts were introduced in 1967. Not a bare majority (as is still the case in Scotland where, rather surprisingly to my mind, an accused can be convicted by a majority of eight to seven) but by eleven to one or ten to two.

Secondly, the ending, although only in certain limited circumstances, of the finality principle, the so-called double jeopardy rule. Until 1996, if a defendant was acquitted by the jury, he went free and could never again be prosecuted for the same offence, however clear it later became that he was guilty or, indeed, that the jury had been bribed or threatened to acquit him. That has now changed. In 1996 provision was made for the quashing of tainted acquittals, where, for example, a juror or witness had been interfered with or intimidated. And in 2005 provision was made for a fresh trial if "new and compelling evidence" had become available since an earlier acquittal.

Can anyone doubt the wisdom of these changes? Was it ever acceptable that a murderer or rapist, once acquitted, was immune from further trial and punishment notwithstanding that, for example, DNA evidence or indeed his own post-acquittal confessions could prove his guilt beyond any possible doubt? I would suggest clearly not, yet there remain old-fashioned civil libertarians who would defend the shibboleth of the double jeopardy rule in its most absolute form to their last breath.

That brings me conveniently to a particular trial without a jury which took place earlier this year amidst a great deal of fierce controversy: the trial of four men for armed robbery and associated firearms offences at a Heathrow warehouse. This, it was widely said, was the first serious criminal trial by judge alone, without a jury, for 400 years, a massive erosion of the accuseds' civil liberties. Consider the basic facts, however. The order dispensing with a jury was made because of evidence of jury intimidation. There had been three earlier attempts at a jury trial. During the first, one of the defendants had had a heart attack. At the second the jury was reduced to nine and was in the end unable to reach a verdict. The third was stopped after allegations of jury tampering.

Those three trials together apparently cost over £20m and, if there was to be a fourth jury trial, the cost of police protection for the jury was alone estimated at a further £6m. And still there would have remained the risk of jury intimidation. In those circumstances the Court of Appeal ordered trial by judge alone. That trial lasted under three months, probably less than half the time a jury trial would have taken. And it resulted in a lengthy reasoned judgment extending to 386 paragraphs.

I do not want to discuss the case in any detail, not least because it may conceivably yet come before us on appeal. But I do want to suggest that it really isn't quite so unique and dramatic a departure from established practice as most commentators have suggested. On the contrary, a close analogy can be seen between this case and the judge alone trials which have been taking place for over thirty years in Northern Ireland in respect of terrorist-related offences during the troubles there – the Diplock Courts as they were known, following their establishment upon the recommendation of a Commission chaired by Lord Diplock.

These too were introduced because of the intimidation of jurors – in Northern Ireland by paramilitary groups. They began in 1973 and lasted until 2007 when, save for an occasional exceptional case, they were abolished. And the odd fact is that, cavil as the purists might at the whole idea of these non-jury trials, no one doubted their absolute fairness in practice. There were many indeed, on both sides of that unhappy sectarian divide, who regarded the Diplock Courts as providing a form of justice altogether superior to that previously available under the jury system.

HAVING GLANCED at the history of juries, having I hope dispelled the myth that they date from Magna Carta, having noticed how dramatically juries have changed down the years, it is high time I cut to the chase. What are their pros, what are their cons? Are they a good idea? To ask that most inelegant of questions: are they fit for purpose in the 21st century?

To answer this question it is, I suggest, necessary first to make up our minds about just what the purpose of jury trials is. Essentially I would suggest that they are intended to serve three purposes: first, to bring in correct verdicts; secondly, to satisfy the public, and indeed the accused, that serious criminal cases are being properly tried and decided – to ensure that justice is not only being done but is being seen to be done; and, thirdly, to give the public a stake in the criminal justice system. Let me consider each of these purposes in turn.

As to the first of them, surely the jury's first and paramount purpose is to do what their oath requires, faithfully to try the defendant and give a true verdict according to the evidence.

Although, as I shall come to explain, I am somewhat sceptical about the jury's record in bringing in correct verdicts, let me at once recognise that very many people take the contrary view and let me acknowledge at the outset certain obvious advantages which juries may be thought to have over professional judges in getting to the right answer.

First and foremost, as a body of twelve, juries are likely to have a broader range of experience and expertise than a single judge. The fact too that they come from a wider social spectrum may give them insights into a variety of situations with which trials are sometimes concerned.

For example, one of the jurors is more likely than the judge to have had some experience of pub brawls or road rage incidents or car boot sales which may variously have led to trials for public order offences, or assault, or receiving of stolen goods. And because of these advantages it might be said that juries are better able than judges to decide certain issues commonly arising in criminal trials such as: was the defendant using no more than reasonable force in his self-defence, or was the defendant dishonest (a concept defined in law partly in terms of community standards of morality and behaviour); or was the defendant not merely negligent but grossly negligent so as to be criminally liable?

All that said, if getting to the right answer means convicting the guilty and acquitting the innocent, I would suggest that juries are not in fact especially good at it. Although not everyone would agree with me, it is certainly my experience that, whilst juries are most unlikely to convict the innocent, they are altogether too prone to acquit the guilty.

Of course, as must be recognised, the whole system is geared to safeguarding the innocent from conviction – better that ten (or is it a hundred?) guilty men go free than that one innocent man be convicted – so that a jury must not convict unless they are sure of the accused's guilt beyond reasonable doubt.

But my experience is that all too often even the patently guilty go free. Maybe this is because the jury fail to see through some smokescreen defence or maybe they are hoodwinked by clever counsel into supposing that there remains room for doubt or maybe they are just not intelligent enough to follow the evidence and see where logically it takes them.

Why is it, one wonders, that magistrates, who of course try roughly 95% of all criminal cases, convict some 70% of those before them, juries at most only some 60%? Some would explain this by reference to the greater difficulty in proving guilt in trials of the more serious crimes – where generally the prosecution have to prove a particular mental state. For example in a case of attempted murder, it must be proved that the accused intended actually to kill the victim.

(It is an oddity of our law that to commit murder you do not have to intend to kill; you need only have intended to cause your victim some really serious injury. If with that intent you kill him, you commit murder. In short you pay for the consequences. Once there is a body, therefore, murder is easier to prove than attempted murder. But that is a digression.)

Others may explain the discrepancy in conviction rates by saying that judges become case-hardened, cynical, too ready to disbelieve what may after all not be a smokescreen but rather a genuine defence – in other words, that judges have a tendency to presume guilt and to convict too readily. Logic, however, tells me otherwise. Surely it stands to reason. Judges are trained by a lifetime's experience to sift and weigh evidence, to analyse the probabilities, to recognise that coincidences are seldom to be found piled one upon another, and that circumstantial evidence is often the most powerful evidence of all – circumstances, unlike witnesses, cannot lie. How can juries, untrained in these skills, and without the judge's ability to read up the details of the case in advance, to keep a full note of the evidence, to study it overnight and so forth, hope to compete?

Small wonder that in some of the more difficult cases juries throw up their hands in despair, feel that there are aspects of the evidence they can never be confident of having really mastered, and retreat behind the shelter of the burden of proof, comforting themselves against any thought that they may be releasing a dangerous criminal or fraudulent menace back onto the streets by reference to the endlessly repeated warning of their need to be absolutely sure of the defendant's guilt before they can convict.

Par excellence this is true in long and complex cases, whether terrorist or fraud trials or indeed almost any substantial case involving for example conflicting expert evidence or other complicated factual material. Although, as I readily acknowledge, it is less true of short and simple cases, concerning, say, street fighting, or shoplifting, or householders defending themselves against burglars, is it really to be supposed that judges themselves are unable to get to the truth in these cases?

Lord Justice Bridge once said:

"In jury trial brevity and simplicity are the hand-maidens of justice, length and complexity its enemies."

Felicitous and true as far as it goes. But it begs rather than answers the question as to whether, even in brief and simple cases (of which, I may say, there are ever fewer) juries are any better than judges in arriving at the correct verdict.

By and large, therefore, on the hugely important question as to whether juries are more likely than judges to reach the right verdicts in the sense of convicting the guilty and acquitting the innocent, I remain unpersuaded that juries are a good idea.

WHAT, THEN, of the appearance of justice, the second important purpose of the jury system?

Here to my mind juries score more heavily. The plain fact is that the public appear to have an altogether greater confidence in a system where the accused's guilt in serious cases is decided not by a professional judge but by a random selection of the accused's fellow citizens.

That apart, jury trial seems in some way to bring closure to cases, to act almost as a catharsis when the social order is disturbed and when, after some of the more notorious crimes, the community appears traumatised. Some see symbolism in the very fact that there are twelve jurors, like the twelve apostles or the twelve tribes of Israel. Some find value in the ritualistic, perhaps even theatrical, nature of the jury trial process: the summoning and swearing of the panel, the jury bailiff's oath as he escorts the jury into retirement for their deliberations, the solemn taking of the verdicts and so forth.

Generally, whatever the jury's eventual verdict may be, the public accept it unquestioningly however inadequately, and therefore misleadingly, the evidence in the case may have been reported by the media covering the trial, And however strongly a convicted defendant may continue to protest his innocence, the public tends usually to have a near absolute faith in the verdict of their fellow citizens, in a way quite different from their reaction to the decisions of professional judges.

I should mention at this point another aspect of jury trial which a lot of people think important: the jury's ability if they think fit actually to ignore the law, indeed to defy the law – jury equity or jury nullification as this is sometimes called. Some would question whether in truth this is an advantage rather than a disadvantage of jury trial. Such a notion is, after all, essentially anarchic, conflicting head on with the rule of law. But most think it an advantage, a valuable safety valve in the system, a safeguard against what are perceived as oppressive and unjust laws. At its most dramatic this power of the jury to defy the law affords protection against overweening state power.

That certainly is how it was perceived by De Tocqueville in the 19th century. Describing the jury as "above all a political institution", he pointed out:

The true sanction of political laws is to be found in penal legislation, and if that sanction be wanting the law will sooner or later lose its cogency. He who punishes infractions of the law is therefore the real master of society. Now the institution of the jury raises the people itself to the bench of judicial authority … [A]ll the sovereigns who have chosen to govern by their own authority, and to direct society instead of obeying its directions, have destroyed or enfeebled the institution of the jury. The monarchs of the House of Tudor sent to prison jurors who refused to convict… [and so forth.]

Dictatorship, for sure, is not a present threat in this country. But in the case of crimes against the state, for example treason, sedition, or offences against the Official Secrets Act, jurors provide a valuable reassurance of justice being done. And juries afford protection against other risks of injustice too, for example over-zealous prosecutions (say of those possessing cannabis for medical use), the victimisation of whistle-blowers (most famously the Clive

Ponting case), or excessive censorship (such as the prosecution of *Lady Chatterley's Lover*). And there are various borderline areas of the law calling for particularly sensitive judgments where I think almost everyone would prefer the verdict of a jury to that of a judge.

Take two high-profile cases heard earlier this year, each involving a mother prosecuted for the unlawful killing of her gravely disabled child, superficially similar but in reality far from it. In one the jury convicted and the mother was sentenced to nine years imprisonment. In the other, the mother having earlier pleaded guilty to aiding and abetting her daughter's suicide, the jury acquitted her of attempted murder. Imposing merely a twelve months' conditional discharge, the judge paid tribute to the jury for its "commonsense, decency and humanity" which, he said, "makes jury trials so important in cases of this kind."

I agree. One hopes that judges too have these qualities but it is easier for a jury to acquit without having to explain why than for a judge to give a reasoned judgment justifying a decision which is in reality based upon no more than sound human instincts.

I SHALL HAVE TO return later to the all-important question of reasons but I must move now, if briefly, to the third purpose commonly recognised as being served by jury trial: giving the public a stake in the criminal justice system.

The very fact that jurors are required to play their part in the criminal justice system undoubtedly tends to make them better citizens themselves. Indeed, De Tocqueville described jury service as a "peerless teacher of citizenship". Not only does it heighten the jury's appreciation of the legal framework within which they are required to live their own lives i.e. the need to obey the law lest they find themselves in the unenviable position of the defendant standing trial before them. In addition it gives jurors a real sense of responsibility and involvement in the justice system.

However reluctant jurors may be to serve, almost invariably in retrospect they are proud to have fulfilled their public duty. After jury service a juror can no longer think the world divided into them and us in quite the same way. Of course, he already has his democratic right to vote. But that is merely to decide which party is to constitute "them". In deciding on the guilt or innocence of others he himself has ceased to be exclusively one of "us" and has become instead in some small way one of "them", part of the establishment engaged in the proper ordering of society. As Lord Devlin famously said "Each jury is a little parliament". Jury service is a form of participatory democracy, of National Service, a small scale engagement in governance. The value of the jury system in this respect should not go unrecognised.

I HAVE THUS FAR avoided but must now at last confront what seems to me undoubtedly the greatest single defect in the process of jury trial: the lack of reasons for the jury's verdict.

The fact that juries' verdicts are unreasoned is not a matter of chance or choice; it is in reality an inescapable consequence of the whole system of jury trial. How on earth could twelve disparate people, of mixed experience and mixed intelligence, hope to articulate a coherent, let alone a cogent and convincing, explanation as to how they have assessed the evidence and, in the light of the principles of law upon which they have been directed by the judge in his summing up, as to how they have therefore arrived at their conclusions? One has only to state the problem to recognise its insolubility. Lord Justice Bramwell observed over a century ago: "If juries had to give reasons for their verdict, trial by jury would not last five years." Five years would seem to me an optimistic prognosis: five months more likely.

Jeremy Thorpe amongst others was famously acquitted of conspiracy to murder in a much publicised jury trial in 1979. When the *New Statesman* later interviewed one of the jurors and published his account of how the verdict had been arrived at, it fell to me as counsel for the Attorney General to seek to have the *New Statesman* found guilty of contempt of court for publishing the secrets of the jury room. In doing so I sought to pray in aid the comments of Lord Hewart, the Lord Chief Justice, in a case in 1922:

If one juryman might communicate with the public upon the evidence and the verdict, so might his colleagues also, and if they all took this dangerous course, differences of individual opinion might be made manifest which, at the least, could not fail to diminish the confidence that the public rightly has in the general propriety in criminal verdicts.

Although my contempt application against the *New Statesman* failed, the government immediately enacted the Contempt of Court Act 1981 which by section 8, as I mentioned earlier, prohibits any disclosure of the jury's deliberations.

The result of all this is that juries' verdicts are appealable only on very limited and in reality somewhat artificial grounds. They cannot be attacked, as reasoned judgments of the court ordinarily are, on the basis that the judge wrongly assessed a witness's veracity or reliability, or failed to take proper account of this, that or the other piece of evidence, or came to an illogical conclusion when applying the law to the facts. Rather the jury's verdict is only challengeable on essentially two main bases, neither of which is to my mind entirely satisfactory.

One basis for an appeal against a jury's verdict is if the jury has misbehaved. In centuries past one finds occasional reported cases of jurymen being seen coming to their verdicts by tossing a coin or throwing dice. Rather more astonishingly, as recently as 1994, an appeal was allowed against a conviction on two counts of murder in the following circumstances.

The jury, having retired to consider their verdict, were unable to reach a decision that day and so were accommodated overnight at a local hotel. (Nowadays the strict practice of isolating juries during their retirement has been abandoned and jurors are now allowed home overnight but it was not so then.) During the evening four of the jurors met and conducted a session together with an Ouija board, asking questions of one of the murder victims and purporting to receive his answers. These answers went to the heart of the case and were highly adverse to the accused. After some later discussion at the hotel with the other jurors about the Ouija board session, the jury unanimously convicted on both counts.

The only real difficulty for the Court of Appeal was section 8 of the Contempt of Court Act. Since, however, the jury's stay in the hotel was an interval between jury-room sessions and not, therefore, a period during which the jury as a whole was in the course of its deliberations, it was open to the Court of Appeal to enquire into what had happened at the hotel albeit not what had happened thereafter in the jury room itself after their return to court. Had the Ouija board been brought out, or a coin tossed, in the jury room itself, the court then would have been barred from receiving evidence on the matter and the convictions would accordingly have stood.

The other and of course far more frequent ground for appealing against conviction is that the judge has misdirected the jury upon the law. You will, I think, all of you know the underlying basis of jury trial: the judge is solely responsible for all questions of law and, in his summing up to the jury at the end of the trial, after all the evidence has been heard and both counsel have addressed the jury, the judge tells them everything they need to know about the law: the ingredients of the offence that they are trying, the basis of any defences that may be available, the burden and standard of proof and so on and so forth. If the jury convict, defending counsel then pore over the legal directions in a desperate endeavour to find some error, however minor, or some lack of clarity, or some failure to warn the jury of some particular problem or another, in the hope of eventually being able to persuade the Appeal Court that just possibly the jury might have approached the case in the wrong way.

I MENTIONED at the outset Professor Thomas's recent research into jury trials. Her primary finding was that these disclose no discernible bias on grounds of ethnicity. But one part of her report entitled "Juror comprehension" concerns "judicial directions on the law" and, unsurprisingly to my mind, suggests that a substantial number of jurors in practice have real difficulty in understanding these directions.

Consider just one brief passage describing Professor Thomas's research amongst jurors at Winchester about their understanding of the judge's directions on self defence, hardly one of the most difficult areas of the law. These jurors were asked to identify the two questions the judge had explicitly directed them to answer in determining whether the defendant had acted in self defence – did the defendant believe it was necessary to defend himself and did he use reasonable force?

Professor Thomas found that only 31% of the jurors accurately identified both questions; a further 48% correctly identified one of the two questions; 20% did not correctly identify either question. That is not to say that jurors are necessarily reaching the wrong conclusions. But one suspects, and indeed much anecdotal evidence suggests, that juries often approach their fact-finding role in a very different way from that commended to them in the judge's summing up.

Appeals, therefore, which focus minutely on the precise language used by the judge in the formulation of his legal directions, for all the world as if the jury in their retirement had themselves recalled these directions verbatim and accurately applied them at all stages in their deliberations, seem to me highly artificial. Yet this approach to conviction appeals, unsatisfactory though it may be, is in reality the inescapable consequence of unreasoned jury decisions. The theory is that the reasons for the verdict are to be found in the judge's directions on the law. If the jury convict, that is because they have faithfully followed to the letter all the judge's instructions on the legal principles in play. If the directions were faulty, then of course their verdict cannot stand. But if they were correctly instructed in the law, their verdict on the facts is unimpeachable and well-nigh sacrosanct.

A GROWING BODY of opinion questions the sustainability of this restricted approach to appeals. Prominent amongst the doubters is the European Court of Human Rights in Strasbourg. There are those who think that the real threat to the jury system comes from the domestic front – most obviously perhaps from government, concerned partly at the huge expense of lengthy jury trials, partly at their comparatively low conviction rates. They fondly suppose that the Human Rights Convention will come to their aid in resisting any attempts by government to narrow down the existing scope of jury trial. They could not be more mistaken. The real threat to the jury system lies rather in the Convention itself and above all in the Strasbourg Court's increasing intolerance of unreasoned jury decisions.

Amongst the many cases before the European Court of Human Rights which are of concern to the UK Government, one in particular is causing them the most acute anxiety: *Taxquet v Belgium*. Mr Taxquet was convicted of murder by a Belgian jury and his appeal dismissed by the Belgian Appeal Court. He then complained to Strasbourg that his human rights had been violated, notably his right to a fair trial. This, he said, he had not had since the trial process had denied him a reasoned decision as to why the jury convicted him. His complaint was accepted by a seven-judge chamber of the European Court. I will quote two passages only from their judgment:

In its case-law the Court has frequently held that the reasoning provided in court decisions is closely linked to the concern to ensure a fair trial as it allows the rights of the defence to be preserved. Such reasoning is essential to the very quality of justice and provides a safeguard against arbitrariness. [para 43]

Not having been given so much as a summary of the main reasons why the Assize Court was satisfied that he was guilty, he was unable to understand – and therefore to accept – the court's decision. This is particularly significant because the jury does not reach its verdict on the basis of the case filed but on the basis of the evidence it has heard at the trial. It is therefore important, for the purpose of explaining the verdict both to the accused and to the public at large – the "people" in whose name the decision is given – to highlight the considerations that have persuaded the jury of the accused's guilt or innocence and to indicate the precise reasons why each of the questions has been answered in the affirmative or the negative. [para 48]

At the Belgian Government's request the case was then referred to the Grand Chamber in Strasbourg where it was heard by a panel of seventeen judges last October, exactly a year ago. Although a Belgian case, the governments of the United Kingdom, Ireland and France had all by that stage submitted arguments as interested third parties. Small wonder. It is hardly to be thought that a trial system venerated for centuries not merely in the UK but in a number of other democracies too may be brought down by an international Human Rights Court but until the Grand Chamber finally makes up its mind on the point no one can be certain what the future holds. It would, I think, be surprising if Monsieur Taxquet's case were indeed to spell the end of our long history of trial by jury. But until that verdict is returned there can be no certainty that the jury's fate lies in our own hands. My ruminations this afternoon may yet prove to have been a complete waste of time.

⁂

POSTSCRIPT: Within a comparatively short time of this lecture the Grand Chamber issued their judgment in *Taxquet* reversing the first instance decision of the lower chamber and thus vindicating the legality of trial by jury.

Epilogue

TRULY MINE HAS BEEN a charmed life. What joys and rewards it has provided. And at what little cost; how few sacrifices I have had to make.

With *Second Helpings* now finally served, I hope that I have – in one sense at least, although, importantly, not in another! – made a meal of it. Certainly, however, the table has now been cleared and the washing-up done. There will be no more memoirs, only perhaps one day the odd obituary and just possibly (though personally I would discourage it) a kindly tribute at a memorial service.

At one of the many of these I have attended in recent years, a lovely service in New College chapel for Paul Clarke, a fellow bencher who died much too young, the tribute was given by a lifelong friend, Paul's solicitor. This friend told us that Paul, knowing he was close to death, had asked him to give the oration, preferably not at extravagant cost.

"Don't worry," Paul had added, "it won't be too difficult. I've written it already, and," – handing it over – "here it is!"

To the delight of all present, Paul's own text, admirably witty and self-deprecating, was then duly read out.

But I am, I hope, getting a little ahead of myself. I really want to end this further memoir with the recognition that, not merely have I been hugely fortunate both in my family life down the years – blessed with a happy childhood, a loving and ever supportive wife, three wonderful and remarkable children, all happily married/partnered, who between them have produced five adorable grandchildren – and in my professional life, but also that mine was one of the luckiest generations ever to have sought their fortunes at the Bar.

As I observed earlier (in CHAPTER 5), our particular generation was notably thin on the ground, facing therefore throughout our careers less competition than when later the Bar grew so large. As the years have passed, we have always seemed to keep one step ahead of the game. The image suggested by a colleague of mine is that of our passing through every stage of our lives with massive steel trapdoors slamming shut just behind us.

Since my call to the Bar, I was never summoned for interview, I never had to apply for any post or promotion, I was never required to make a presentation, I never had to provide references, I never had to undertake that most cringe-making of tasks, writing a self-assessment; indeed, I never even had to prepare a c.v. When appointed to the High Court Bench, I could continue till seventy-five albeit needing to serve only fifteen years to retire on a full pension.

Those appointed after 1995 have to retire at seventy and must have served for twenty years to be entitled to a full pension (and that less generous than under our generation's scheme). On reaching the final appeal court, I and my colleagues all became members of the House of Lords; our successors in the Supreme Court are granted only courtesy titles.

Over the years, moreover, life for both the Bar and the Bench seems to me to have become more onerous, more earnest, more challenging, altogether less fun than it used to be.

Whilst revelling in my own good fortune, however, I do not wish to dishearten those who follow. Despite all I've said, there is still, I feel sure, romance and magic in store for some at least of those irresistibly drawn to the Bar. It remains without question an honourable profession. Upon it, and upon the independent judiciary it feeds, depends the rule of law, the very lifeblood of our liberal democracy. Few in the future may expect to experience quite the same extraordinary degree of luck and satisfaction that I enjoyed. But for some at least I trust that the trapdoors may open and that they too may come to enjoy as charmed a life as I have had.

Last Scrapings

THIS END SECTION *(its title suggested by Jenny) consists of thirteen disparate pieces written since the publication of* Second Helpings *in hardback. Clearly no third volume of memoirs could possibly be justified. But I thought these pieces just about worth preserving. Three of them have previously appeared in print elsewhere: "Sleeping in Court" somewhat shortened in the* Oldie, *"Golf on Circuit" in* Golf Quarterly, *and "Legal Legends" in the* Middle Templar. *"Launching Beloff" is the introductory speech I gave at the launch of* his *memoir.*

These assorted pieces may, I hope, variously interest or amuse some at least of those acquiring this now expanded second volume of my own memoirs.

CHAPTER I

The Mont Cervin

W HEN in 1963 I joined 2 Garden Court Chambers and moved into Bill Macpherson's room, I soon noticed, amongst Bill's briefs lined up on the mantelpiece, one entitled *Clarkson Booker Ltd v Ronald Albuquerque Andjel*.

Ronnie Andjel, though not his second name, Albuquerque, I knew from Oxford. He had been a prominent figure in my time there: a larger-than-life character, a little older than most of us, highly sociable, a somewhat exotic undergraduate at Jesus, an unfashionable college (*pace* my old friend Bruce Markham David who over long years has delighted all those who have encountered him). Ronnie was inevitably to be seen at any large Oxford party – and in our time, the late 1950s, these were legion – invariably at the heart of the action and, indeed, if gambling was afoot, at its very epicentre. He was undoubtedly charming and amusing and no party would have been complete without him. But he was also thought by many something of a chancer and the wiser amongst the undergraduates of his acquaintance, male as well as female (a distinction in those days not thought difficult to make), would treat him a little warily. He was, indeed, known to some, if perhaps unfairly, as "Ron the Con".

I need not dwell on the Clarkson Booker case. It arose out of a travel business Ronnie had set up (begun, I recall, whilst still at Oxford) renting out holiday villas, and it involved a rather arcane point of agency law, the contractual liability of undisclosed principals. Ronnie found himself at the wrong end of the judgments, both at first instance and on appeal. Bumping into him as occasionally I did after Oxford, I well recall him saying more than once that if only he'd had Bill Macpherson acting on his side rather than against him he'd have won the case. But I had little doubt that was nonsense. Certainly Bill was more to Ronnie's taste as a robust, no-frills advocate than his rather more cerebral opponent, Adrian Hamilton (a not surprising distinction given their Oxford legal education respectively at Trinity and Balliol). But this was not the kind of dispute to be resolved by differing styles of advocacy. I should, I think, add in all fairness that Ronnie went on to have a successful career in business, centred I believe on property.

The point of this piece, however, is not that case nor, indeed, Ronnie's prominence generally on the Oxford undergraduate scene. Rather it is the part he played in what I confess is a story deeply to the discredit of several undergraduates, myself not least.

It is a story set in the ski resort of Zermatt. Twice as a teenager I had been taken there by my parents during school holidays and an enchanting place it then was. In those long-ago days the only skiing was on the Gornergrat, the Gornergrat mountain railway the only route to the higher slopes. And in those days the village itself, accessible only by rail up from Visp in the Rhône valley below, was serviced by a single battery-powered vehicle. Today, as indeed for many years past, things are very different. Other adjacent mountain ranges have been opened up for ski runs and Zermatt itself is now almost a metropolis, its streets lined with fashionable shops and thronged with numerous motorised vehicles (though still happily not private cars).

Back, however, to the Oxford Christmas vacation of 1959. Four of us from Worcester had rented a small self-catering chalet. A much larger group, some two dozen strong, including sundry girlfriends, gathered up by Ronnie who thereby himself went free, were also there, staying in more luxurious staffed accommodation.

Besides the monolithic Zermatterhof hotel (where my parents had first taken me), there was just one other stylish hotel, the Mont Cervin, which on Friday nights had a terrific Italian dance band. And there it was that we four went on our last evening, finding already assembled, and joining up with, Ronnie's larger group.

Little of the evening do I now, over sixty years on, recall in any detail. Really only its deplorable ending, seared on the memory.

Throughout the evening drinks were periodically ordered and consumed, though not I think excessively or extravagantly, with the bill chits steadily accumulating in a glass on the central table. (Unlike in England, payment is habitually made on the continent not round by round but in total at the end.) I do not recall any arrangement having been made for the eventual payment of this bill. Rather I recall only that, as the evening wore on, at some point it struck me that ours was a gradually diminishing group, its members slowly drifting away into the night. Realising at that stage that not all would be making any contribution to the final joint bill, I looked around to ask Ronnie what he proposed doing about this. As my readers will doubtless have guessed, Ronnie was by then nowhere to be seen. He was amongst those who had already left.

Now, I fear, must come my own confession. It was then that I myself decided to join the surreptitious exodus. Shameful and lamentable though of course I now recognise this to have been, the alternative at the time seemed alarming: the few of us remaining would be picking up a hefty bill we could ill afford with little prospect of ever recovering any part of it from the departed others (all of us leaving for England the next morning).

Who at that point was left? Were any of the three others in my own small group? What, if anything, happened at the end? Did anyone make any payment towards the bill? None of this for the life of me can I now recall. I am left only with the abiding memory of having myself shamelessly walked away.

Famously, asked during a TV interview what was the naughtiest thing she had ever done in her youth, our then Prime Minister, Teresa May, answered: "running through a field of wheat". Infamously, my own answer would have had to have been: "bilking a foreign hotel". I should have found it an uncomfortable admission to make.

❧

BY WAY OF postscript I add this. After completing the above piece I sent it to one of the other three in our group (Iain Mackintosh, a fellow Garrick member), asking for any recollections of that last evening he might have. He said it rang no bells whatever; indeed his sole memory of the entire holiday was of the water-heater in our chalet being unable to provide for more than a single small daily bath which after skiing we all had to share, taking in turn who went first. Am I, therefore, merely hallucinating about that last evening? I would love to think so. But I fear it has troubled my conscience too continuously for too long to have been mere invention.

CHAPTER 2

Gambling

A NY APPETITE I might ever have had for the excitements of gambling I lost one night in my early adult life some sixty years ago. In retrospect I was lucky that night though it did not seem so at the time. Let me set the scene.

Embarrassing though such an admission now seems, I had a rich grandmother who lived in some style in Bournemouth with two resident maids. She also employed a chauffeur, named Geary, to maintain and drive her elderly Rolls. I went when I could for Sunday lunch and invariably on such occasions she served both a whole roast duck and a roast sirloin of beef and whatever was left of each was then given to Geary to sustain him during the following week.

Come late 1960, I was between Bar Finals and my pupillage year and the family assigned to me the task of accompanying Granny and her companion (another elderly lady selected for the purpose) to the South of France to settle them for the winter until kinder weather returned to Bournemouth.

We flew to Nice, they first class, I tourist, and on arrival duly picked up the pre-hired chauffeured Citroën, theirs for the two or three months of the stay. I was to be with them for just a week, wending our way along the coast, staying a night here, a night there, looking for some niche hotel where they might feel comfortable and at home for the duration. The details of all this I have long since forgotten but memories linger: of the Citroën, so well-sprung it seemed to be riding the waves, sleep coming easily on the longer stretches. And on every journey Granny repeatedly exclaiming: "Oh, do smell the mimosa, isn't it divine?"

Eventually, we decided on a charming little hotel on the seafront at Beaulieu-sur-Mer and it was there that I finally left them.

All this, however, is essentially by the way, merely the backdrop to this story, of my suddenly acquired aversion to gambling. How that came about now at last follows.

On our second night in Cannes, the two old ladies were set on an evening in, with embroidery and cards to hand. After dinner, therefore, it was decided that I should go off and see something of the town. To this end Granny gave me a twenty-franc note, suggesting I might find my way to the casino (this of course long before anything of this kind became legal in England). I was suitably attired: black tie was in those days de rigueur for dinner in the better hotels along the Riviera.

Naturally the casino is where I immediately went, wide-eyed with wonder at its sheer grandeur. Undertaking a brief exploration of this glittering palace, I should perhaps confess to having encountered and sought to chat up quite the prettiest of girls – until, that is, her much older and decidedly threatening consort came swiftly up and, with no attempt at finesse whatever, sent me abashedly upon my way. I then made for the cheapest of the roulette tables and stood around it for a while observing the play. The lowest permitted stake was two francs (worth then some £4 sterling today). I duly exchanged my note for ten such chips and took a place at the table. Really no elaboration is necessary of what then followed. Quite simply, I placed ten successive two-franc bets at evens (variously by numbers and colours) and, without interruption, lost every single one. My evening's entertainment was thus concluded in but little over half an hour. Any attraction I might otherwise have felt for the thrill of the spinning wheel instantly dissolved. And never have I been tempted since.

That night I returned to our hotel thinking myself to have been the unluckiest man in the world. It took me some years to realise what I now know, that on the contrary I had been quite the luckiest.

CHAPTER 3

An Open and Shut Case

I'VE ONLY EVER been twice to the Isle of Wight. Once, comparatively recently, for a 70th birthday party, a most enjoyable but otherwise unremarkable event. The first time, however, now over half a century ago, was in my earliest years at the Bar when, more memorably, I went to defend a sassy young East End girl on a charge of shoplifting. We had arranged to meet on the ferry across to the island to discuss her defence, the day having begun at what had been for me a disagreeably early hour and with a brief fee almost certain to be exceeded by my travel expenses – a not uncommon experience in those days and still, according to some members of the criminal Bar recently on strike, not unknown today.

The basic facts of the case were that on the day of the alleged offence my client had gone to the island to visit her boyfriend in Parkhurst prison and then later, on her way back to the ferry, had called in at a boutique clothes shop close to the port, where she had tried on two or three dresses before finally leaving empty-handed. I say "empty-handed" but it was common ground that throughout the day she had with her a zip-up carrier bag, the critical issue being whether at that stage it contained a stolen dress.

The case against her consisted essentially of two pieces of evidence. First, that after her departure, but not soon enough to track her down before she boarded the ferry, one of the dresses she had been trying on in the cubicle had been found to be missing. Secondly, it was the shop assistant's evidence that whilst the defendant was in the cubicle she (the witness) heard the carrier bag being unzipped.

The defence was a straightforward denial. The defendant strongly denied having taken a dress and denied also having opened up her bag whilst in the shop.

What, however, down all the years has stuck most indelibly in my memory is the terms in which, as we discussed her defence during the crossing to the island on the morning of her trial, my client had fortified her denial of the suggestion that she had been heard whilst in the cubicle opening or closing the zip of her bag. As to this, she told me:

"I was taught (shoplifting) by Alfie Hinds' mother and they don't come better than that. If I *had* operated the zip there is no way anyone could possibly have heard it."

Alfie Hinds, I should add for those too young to recall that long-past era, was a notorious (or perhaps I should say celebrated) burglar of the time, renowned above all for a succession of brazen prison escapes.

As to my handling of my client's case, although to my mind this account of her tutoring was easily the most compelling feature of her defence, it was not evidence which I thought it wise to deploy before the Isle of Wight Magistrates. Fortunately, however, for my client, if not perhaps for the wider interests of justice, the Bench on balance found the case not proved to the required standard and so acquitted her. Congratulating her upon the result, and noting that she was booked that evening on a late ferry home, I confined myself to suggesting that it might perhaps be sensible for her to avoid visiting any more shops before finally leaving the island.

CHAPTER 4

Sweat

OR MOST OF my adult life I suffered from a most excruciatingly embarrassing physical ailment, profuse sweatiness. I describe it as a physical ailment because that is how it manifested itself. But it was generally precipitated not by any sort of physical exertion (this is not about vigorous games of squash) but rather for what must have been psychological reasons: a feeling of mental pressure, perhaps allied to a sudden failure of self-confidence.

It was liable to happen in a variety of different circumstances but most especially when I felt in the spotlight: in court, in conference, in close conversation, giving a lecture, even merely at some social event. And, once started, one's embarrassment, and indeed one's consciousness of its almost invariable progression, instantly accelerated and exacerbated its intensity.

I should make plain that I am not here talking about a mere few beads of perspiration which simply require wiping away. Rather a positive fountain of sweat, breaking out all over, including cascading down from the forehead to the extent of clouding one's spectacles, making it impossible to read, melting one's collar (however stiffly starched), and soaking one's shirt and underwear to the point of acute discomfort, for all the world as if they'd been put on wringing wet.

Lest it be thought I exaggerate, let me recall a lecture, not extemporised but with a carefully prepared script, where, quite inexplicably, halfway through, I suffered one of these sweaty outpourings sufficient to dampen the written pages to the very limits of legibility, despite having paused to dry my glasses.

I recognise, of course, that the sense of embarrassment, and indeed shame, I felt on these occasions at the spectacle I was presenting was excessive, by no means justified by whatever embarrassment or even distaste those witnessing it might be feeling. But the plain fact is that this recurrent phenomenon cast a dismal pall over many years of my professional life and I would have given a great deal to end it. The only conceivable positive to take from this was that it sharpened still further my natural inclination to prepare fully for all engagements.

&

I ONLY EVER knew one other person to suffer from the same affliction. Or at least he claimed to suffer it and certainly on occasion he would appear a touch damp, though I never thought he came within measurable distance of my own capacity for sogginess. This was Pat Russell, a towering Lancastrian whom I eventually came to know well as a fellow judge and Middle Temple Bencher. He was at one time chairman of Lancashire CCC and, in the late 1980s, he took me whilst on circuit in Manchester to the Old Trafford Test match. It was a filthy wet day which allowed, I recall, a bare twenty minutes of seeing the Indians in the field. But the Board lunch which followed was gargantuan and itself amply justified the outing.

Pat, sweaty or not, was an outstandingly able and popular judge. Douglas Brown, one of Pat's close friends also appointed to the High Court from the North West (most of these, like Pat himself, destined to die far too young, though Chris Rose happily remains amongst us) told me of an occasion when the two of them were chatting about the prospects of Pat's judicial promotion.

"They'll never ask me," said Pat, "and if they do I'll refuse."

"Here's £10," Douglas replied, "that says they will and you won't."

It wasn't long before Douglas was entertaining Pat at a smart restaurant at the latter's expense – which says something about subsequent inflation as well as Pat's innate modesty.

I am tempted to recall too an occasion when we had Pat to dinner at home. Having heard him in the Middle Temple a while before say that the one thing he couldn't stomach was venison, when on arrival he sniffed appreciatively and asked what we were having, I mischievously told him "venison". His response was a wan smile with which I left him before returning after a brief moment to say that after all the venison seemed to have turned into beef; I hoped that was all right.

His relief was palpable!

⁂

ALL THAT, however, is essentially by the way. This chapter is about sweating.

Why do I now choose to recall, and indeed actually record, this most embarrassing feature of my own past life? In part because happily it now really does seem securely past – its impact seemingly having lessened as I ascended the judicial hierarchy, hardly therefore ascribable to an "imposter syndrome" as some might suggest! But more particularly because I am now striving to identify such positive improvements wrought by the passage of time in the quality of life as can compensate in some small measure for the overall deterioration. How many of those nightmarish sweats would I now tolerate to restore, for example, my ability to enjoy buggy-free golf? Not perhaps all that many: they really were mortifying. As now the ledger's debit column grows ever longer, it is perhaps the more satisfying to recall such problems of one's prime as no longer persist.

And my final reason is honestly this: memoirs mostly make one out to have been quite a guy, enviably successful and admired, happy as could be in one's own skin. It is surely salutary for the reader to recognise that virtually everyone will have had some, usually unspoken, cross to bear, and that in truth one's own life is unlikely to contrast as disappointingly with the memoirist's as at first blush may have appeared. That realisation may prove a reassurance to some at least of my readers.

CHAPTER 5

Police Truncheons

THE OLD BAILEY half a century ago was a frightening place to appear in. And that was just if you were defence counsel. For the defendants it was obviously worse still. The Old Bailey judges of that time were a notoriously harsh bunch. Names like Edward Clarke, Michael Argyll and Gwyn Morris spring to mind. But there were exceptions and one of those was Judge Maude QC.

John Maude boasted certain aristocratic connections and, whether or not on that account, was inclined on occasion to somewhat quixotic utterances. Sentencing an accused to prison for an act of gross indecency in a public place, Judge Maude said that not merely had his conduct been utterly loathsome but it had been made all the worse by taking place beneath the arches of Waterloo Bridge, one of London's most lovely bridges.

In another case, here in more merciful mood, addressing a defendant whom he was placing on probation following a string of tiresome, if rather petty, offences, all brought about by his having been drinking to excess, the judge counselled:

"Now, my good man, it is essential that during this year of probation you abstain totally from all alcoholic liquor. Do you understand me? Absolutely no drink whatever, not even the tiniest glass of dry sherry before Sunday luncheon."

These stories, I should confess, have been told before. But now let me add to them a further instance from one of my own appearances before John Maude back in the 1970s. I was defending a well-known London rogue whom finally the police had arrested for a series of burglaries, robberies and the like. The prosecution were determined to throw the book at him and in this instance "the book" included a charge, albeit rather less serious than most of the others, of receiving stolen goods, namely a Metropolitan Police truncheon found in his possession on arrest.

The evidence of this truncheon having been stolen consisted solely in the fact that no one save a serving police officer could be in lawful possession of it: these weapons had to be strictly accounted for within the force.

The police witness from whom prosecuting counsel was endeavouring to elicit this essential piece of evidence was proving singularly obtuse, not readily seeing that what was required of him was to set out the accounting procedures in place. Growing visibly impatient, the judge decided to take the matter into his own hands:

"Now officer, what we need to understand is how a police constable comes to get one of these truncheons. Are there police stores from which they are issued individually and signed for? Or does a newly recruited officer simply pop down the road to Harrods and ask the sales staff for one at the counter there?"

At this point unsurprisingly the penny dropped and this aspect of the prosecution's case was neatly tied up. So too were almost all the other charges.

I have long forgotten the length of prison sentence to which my client was subjected (I have no doubt it was richly deserved and doubt it was any longer on account of the police truncheon) and nor do I remember the details of any of the more serious offences of which he was convicted. But as long as I live I shall never forget the striking suggestion that perhaps what new Metropolitan Police officers in need of a truncheon must do is just "pop down the road to Harrods".

CHAPTER 6

Beards *vs* Pupils

D URING THE PANDEMIC a great many men grew a beard. I was amongst them, sprouting a growth to eke out the dwindling thatch above. And I have kept it, largely because persuaded by my grandchildren. This, like so much else in these changed times, prompted musings of times past. I could not, for example, resist comparing today's shabby grey stubble with the vigorous dark beard I was so proudly displaying at the age of twenty-one in the photograph at page 46 of *Playing off the Roof*, my earlier memoir.

That, however, is not a comparison to dwell on. I prefer rather to move on a few years, to when I was in practice at the Bar, following the sartorial conventions of those days: black bowler hats, starched white collars and pinstripe trousers. Clean-shaven myself (like the vast majority of young barristers), I made it a rule never to take a bearded applicant into pupillage. What, I used to wonder, did the beard signify? Almost certainly some tiresomely combative spirit.

So it was that when, in the mid 1970s, a young Richard Davies applied, aggressively bearded, for pupillage with me, I instantly rejected him, candidly explaining why (not, obviously, an explanation one could get away with today). But I was happy to give him a cup of tea and we chatted. He had, it speedily became clear (and

in truth the beard bore it out), a fiercely radical political outlook;
had, indeed, recently been sent down from Liverpool University,
where he'd been president of the union, for leading (with Jon Snow,
later an institution at Channel Four News) a sit-in student strike,
I forget about what. He was, however, sufficiently keen to become
my pupil that, to my astonishment, he expressly offered to shave
beforehand if I'd take him. Having already warmed to him and
recognised that he was both clever and interesting, likely to prove
stimulating if perhaps challenging company (these initial thoughts
amply borne out in later times), I then and there accepted him on
this basis, exacting a clear promise that he would remain clean-
shaven throughout his year with me.

He proved an excellent pupil, becoming much liked and highly
rated by all in Chambers (then only some fifteen strong at 2 Garden
Court, now a legal powerhouse, ten times that number, 39 Essex
Chambers in Chancery Lane). At the end of his pupillage we
immediately, therefore, took him on as a tenant. But carelessly I
had overlooked the need to renew his promise to remain beard-
less. And from that day to the day he died in November 2008 (far
too young, though already by then having been Head of Chambers
and a most successful and popular silk) he never again appeared
clean-shaven.

Who knows, but for my absurd and outrageous earlier demand,
he might well have abandoned the beard at some point. But frankly
whether that was so or not I had long since ceased to care.

&

THAT EARLY RECOLLECTION of Richard has led inexorably
to another, some thirty years later, shortly after Richard's sad,
and dreadfully premature, death, when I was asked to give the

2009 PIBA (Personal Injury Bar Association) annual lecture in his memory. It is unnecessary to relate its subject, let alone its substance. Rather I shall confine myself to what I said about Richard in my introduction to the lecture.

Having observed how daunting it was to be giving this prestigious lecture in any event, I said how much more so it would have been had Richard actually been there in person. Ever one of my sternest critics, the privilege perhaps of a past pupil, I had no doubt he would have found many holes to pick in what was to follow. But I could not resist observing that not all his criticisms were well-founded, citing in support the case of *Charter Reinsurance v Fagan*. That well-known commercial case turned on an issue of contractual construction, the reinsurer's liability there kicking in only in respect of losses which the reinsured had "actually paid".

Giving the lead judgment in the Court of Appeal (Christopher Staughton dissenting) in 1995, I held that in that context "actually paid" (which, given that the reinsured had gone into liquidation, it probably never would be) also could mean "payable". Richard, with characteristic pugnaciousness said it was one of the most dishonest judgments he'd ever read and that it couldn't possibly survive the pending appeal to the House of Lords.

We struck a £1 bet, the want of confidence implicit in the stake being, I recall, on my part, not his. Dishonest or not, however, all five of their Lordships in 1996 saw it my way and Richard ruefully handed over the £1. He did not, however, cease to excoriate my judgment; he merely included the House of Lords in his withering condemnation.

Clean-shaven or bearded, Richard would have become a notable adornment to the Bench and the cause of justice was amongst many interests which suffered as a result of his premature death.

৯়

RICHARD was one of my six pupils who were then taken on as tenants in Chambers (or in one case later returned there). Each enhanced Chambers' reputation and, no less importantly, contributed hugely to the friendly and stimulating atmosphere which has always characterised the set.

This chapter, principally of course devoted to Richard Davies, provides an irresistible opportunity to say a final few words also about the other five. I take them in no particular order.

৯়

DAVID MELVILLE was Granville Wingate's son-in-law, Granville himself being the revered Head of Chambers on my arrival (and effectively the founder of the chambers in its modern form, a father figure whose practice far outshone any others there and who personally paid the bulk of Chambers' expenses). I was honoured that he asked me to take David, but delighted too: we enjoyed the happiest of years together and he was then unhesitatingly kept on in Chambers where he duly prospered, taking silk and eventually leaving for the Circuit Bench in his beloved West Country, a member of the Garrick and still most happily married to Granville's daughter, Catharine.

৯়

JOHN LAWS was really Bill Macpherson's pupil but, when Bill took silk partway through John's pupillage year, he was then transferred to me, all very conveniently since Bill and I shared a room. This was not a stage in John's illustrious career that he ever found it necessary to mention in later years, clearly regarding it as having diminished rather than enhanced the value of a pupillage with

Bill. Some years later, as Treasury Devil, I sometimes came to lead John (by then himself on the panel of Treasury Counsel) in cases for the Crown. But I confess to never having felt entirely comfortable doing so: he was a notably better lawyer and, I fear, a better advocate than I ever was. Indeed, if to my mind John had a fault (apart from a lamentable fondness for lurid ties and elaborate double-breasted lapelled waistcoats ill-suited to his somewhat portly figure), it was that he never sufficiently sought to disguise the fact that this was clearly his view too.

John, of course, succeeded me as Treasury Devil, an office he loved and filled with distinction. As I remarked in my earlier memoir, he must surely be one of the most brilliant judges never to have been appointed to the House of Lords or Supreme Court. Some are lucky to get there; John was singularly unlucky not to.

ò▲

RICHARD WILMOT-SMITH was a charming and assiduous pupil but happy to accept a tenancy in specialist building contract chambers where he made his name and a fortune. Many years later, and long after I myself had left for the Bench, Richard returned to Chambers, establishing building work as a substantial area of work there. Besides writing an authoritative textbook on the subject, and becoming for many years a most popular Head of Chambers, he finally peaked as Master Treasurer of the Middle Temple.

Beyond all these attainments, however, I would rank highest having fathered three most gifted children: Antonia, a leading mathematician, Claudia, a shipping barrister, and Fred, a prize fellow of All Souls, a peerless young man of limitless charm and ability, now at the Bar following a decade in academe, and destined for glittering forensic success.

ROBERT JAY arrived with a brilliant first from New College and, after a predictably successful year's pupillage, clearly merited a tenancy. This, however, I stupidly nearly cost him, flippantly remarking at the Chambers meeting that it was high time we took on someone really clever, not a remark that endeared me, or indeed him, to the younger members.

As I proudly boasted in my original memoir, Robert later acted as the hugely impressive leading counsel to Brian Leveson's long inquiry into press misconduct and regulation. Truly, he emerged from this as an iconic figure, assured of appointment to the High Court whenever he chose. This duly followed as did several years on the Bench, winning many well-deserved plaudits along the way. Until, catastrophically, he came to try a defamation case brought by a litigant in person who tried Robert's patience to (or, as successive appeal courts later held, beyond) breaking point, so that ultimately an appeal against his judgment was allowed in excoriating terms. Robert immediately then withdrew an application he had earlier made for promotion to the Court of Appeal.

Having read all the judgments in the case, I can only say that I hope still to be around when Robert secures, as surely he must, his further preferment. Really he is far too able a lawyer, and too creative a judge, to spend his whole judicial career at first instance. Moreover, I cannot help reflecting that had judicial patience, extending indeed to patent indulgence of obsessive lay litigants, been regarded as an essential attribute of the High Court Bench in my day, the senior appeal courts would then have looked very different. Indeed, it is highly doubtful whether my own memoirs would have extended much beyond their initial chapters.

પ્ર

EDWIN GLASGOW featured in my earlier memoir, though largely relative to his early years in Chambers. Truly he has proved a king amongst men. He, indeed, together with his great friend and contemporary, Nigel Pleming (whose only deficiency was to find pupillage elsewhere than with me), have constituted the bedrock of Chambers for now over half a century. Each has long since completed a spell as Head of Chambers. Both are pre-eminent amongst the Bar's most successful and admired silks, each, like Granville Wingate before them, having steadfastly declined offers of appointment to the High Court Bench, recognising that there is more to life than mere judicial preferment and the baubles that go with it. Both, however, have made signal contributions elsewhere to the wider public good. Whilst such as Edwin and Nigel continue to set the tone, 39 Essex Chambers will remain the prosperous and happy set it has now long since been recognised to be.

CHAPTER 7

Golf on Circuit

H IGH COURT JUDGES on circuit are often given the
courtesy of golf clubs near their lodgings. It is a huge privilege
and benefit and, in my eight years on that court (almost half spent
on circuit), I made extensive use of it. Not least was this so during
two long summers in Norwich where we were allowed to play at
three clubs: the nearby Royal Norwich, the renowned Royal West
Norfolk at Brancaster, and Bungay (a charming heather course,
Suffolk's answer to Woking).

During the first of my visits to Norwich, one round in particular stands out in the memory, a game at Brancaster with that most
delightful of Lord-Lieutenants, Tim Colman, enlisted for the
purpose by the then High Sheriff, the no-less-delightful Lord
Edward Fitzroy, himself a non-golfer. What made it memorable was not the golf itself, at best indifferent and eminently
forgettable, but rather that the High Sheriff acted as my caddie.
Caddies have been a rarity in my golfing life, a High Sheriff in
that role unique.

An altogether less pleasing memory was left by an outing to
the Royal Norwich course one evening after court. I had taken my
non-golfing marshal (whom I equipped with a single club and a

couple of golfballs) with the aim of enjoying a few holes together for a bit of fresh air and exercise. We were not, of course, competing or even, indeed, scoring. At one particular hole, therefore, having driven into the rough and with no interest in attempting to hack the ball out, I simply kicked it into a good a lie for the next shot. It so happened, however, that at that very moment a fourball was advancing up the fairway opposite.

"Oi", shouted one of the four who had observed me, "I saw that. That's cheating! You can't improve your lie in the rough."

He was not, I may say, easily persuaded that my "opponent" really wouldn't mind.

This recollection still comes back whenever, playing at my home course, Denham, I invoke the Burns Rules (their author Terry, Lord Burns, being one of our somewhat elderly group). Under these rules, summer or winter, fairway or semi-rough, we allow ourselves preferred lies. Golf, after all, is for pleasure and, at our age, where is the pleasure in hitting a poor shot merely because a malignant fate has decreed a rotten lie? We hit quite enough poor shots anyway. With my experience at Royal Norwich still vivid, I nevertheless take pains to ensure that when improving my lie under the Burns Rules, no one outside our regular group sees what is happening. After sixty years of membership, it would be a pity to be thought a cheat by my many friends at Denham.

❧

THERE IS PERHAPS one other aspect of golf on circuit in those days that I should mention. Once, sitting at Newcastle, my wife came up from London for a dinner and was to meet me at court. My list having collapsed, however, she was told that I had gone off with the High Sheriff to play golf at Gosforth (an excellent course weaving around the Newcastle racecourse) and that she should meet me there instead.

Arriving at Gosforth, she was driven from pillar to post, banished successively from the bar, the lounge, the veranda, the clubhouse generally, and finally, the ultimate indignity, the outside terrace. She could seek us out on the course, she was told, or wait in the car park.

Gosforth was not alone in those days in applying this remorselessly anti-women approach. The story used to be told of a member, about to play with his wife one sleepy summer afternoon on an empty seaside course, as they were pulling their golf trolleys over to the first tee, being hailed by a fellow member:

"Ah, Tony, I see you're alone. Would you care for a game?"

Thankfully, errant golf clubs like these have long since put that history behind them.

CHAPTER 8

Sleeping in Court

SUDDEN OVERPOWERING drowsiness, the compulsive clos-
ing of the eyelids, is an almost unstoppable force. Usually it doesn't
matter. Of course it may mean you miss the one news story you
actually turned on the TV to watch, or never discover who was
the killer in the serial you had so avidly been following. But you
can generally catch up later and anyway who cares?

When, however, it really does matter is if you're driving. One
of the saddest cases I ever tried involved a multiple pile-up on
the M1. A lorry driver fell asleep, allowing his vehicle to veer into
a stationary line of traffic queuing to leave the motorway. There
was an instant conflagration and several people died. The charge
was manslaughter, the question for the jury, whether the driver
knew of his propensity to sudden compulsive sleep. They found
he did and a term of seven years followed.

Ever since then, whenever the merest hint of drowsiness has
overtaken me at the wheel, I have found the nearest service station
or exit and stopped. Usually sleep comes almost at once. Putting
the seat back, peremptorily banishing any children, and turning on
Classic FM, all help. And ten minutes later one awakes thoroughly
refreshed.

Happily, however, sleepiness was never a problem which afflicted
me on the Bench. Maybe that was just my good luck. Maybe it was

because I used to participate in proceedings rather more directly than I should have done, probably asking too many questions.

Some judges, however, did have a problem. Lord Denning in his later years, invariably on the dot of 3 p.m., would sleep for five minutes precisely, then wake up sharper than ever so that only the briefest recapitulation was required. But Denning was in his eighties. Other judicial sleepers had less excuse: they by definition were under seventy-five; Tom was the only judge unaffected by the compulsory retirement age – the age of "statutory senility" as Lord Bridge resentfully called it.

Although, as stated, I personally never fell asleep on the Bench, I need to confess to some embarrassment when myself giving the court's judgment one afternoon in the Court of Criminal Appeal and hearing the all too audible snores of my presiding judge as I wound my wearisome way through an interminably (though I would argue necessarily) lengthy recitation of the facts.

THIS RECOLLECTION has reminded me of the only story I ever heard to the undoubted credit of that somewhat contentious circuit judge in Yorkshire, Judge Pickles, newphew of the great Yorkshire broadcaster of my boyhood, Wilfred ("Give 'im the money, Barney") Pickles.

Defending counsel, making his closing speech to the jury, turns to Pickles, the presiding judge:

"I don't know whether Your Honour has noticed, but one of the jurymen is asleep."

"So he is," says the judge. "Well, Mr Green. You put him to sleep, so you'd better wake him up again!"

Judge Pickles was a notoriously savage sentencer, a fact wittily invoked by the circuit leader, Gilly Gray QC, speaking at the North East circuit's two-hundreth anniversary dinner:

"Two hundred years, Mr Junior, two hundred years." (Pause.) "One of Judge Pickles's lighter sentences!"

ᘔ

BUT IT IS time to return to the topic of sleepiness on the Bench and to recount what was far and away the most troubling instance of this I can recall. It was of a hot summer's afternoon, sitting in the Court of Appeal in one of the Royal Courts of Justice's then newly commissioned Crypt Courts. John Balcombe was presiding, Peter Gibson and I his wingers.

I forget what arcane point of chancery law we were addressing but around mid-afternoon I suddenly heard a most disturbing sound. It was of John snoring loudly and, glancing round, I saw him to be out to the world. Not only were those courts low-ceilinged and hot but the Bench was unusually and embarrassingly close to where the lawyers sat facing us. And not only was John snoring loudly but one or two of the lawyers were sniggering.

The situation was intolerable. Naturally I did my best to try to wake John discreetly, initially by raising my voice and asking counsel a series of (needless) questions, then by noisily dropping a heavy volume of law reports on the Bench between us. But none of this had the least effect. Eventually therefore I had no alternative but to lean across, tug John's arm and ask him whether he was feeling all right.

Finally waking at this point, the poor man was suffused with embarrassment, looking guiltily around like a child caught raiding the chocolate box. Nothing, however, was said and the hearing continued to its conclusion, judgment then being reserved.

John himself was to have written the judgment, the point at issue being squarely within his expertise. But having regard to the incident just recorded, Peter and I felt this might not after all be such a good idea. The task, therefore, fell to Peter, the other chancery judge on the court. Writing the judgment would have been well beyond my own competence.

⁂

I END WITH one other recollection of audible snores in court. Regrettably these emanated from my elderly father on the single occasion he came to court to witness his son's forensic brilliance. It is a salutary reminder that not all legal trials are feasts of advocacy, nor alas do all sons invariably live up to their father's expectations.

CHAPTER 9

Legal Legends

Y EARS AGO, when on occasion I was the guest speaker at a college or university's annual law dinner, I used sometimes to begin my speech by self-deprecatingly contrasting my own modest career with that of one of the legal giants of yesteryear. Initially I chose F. E. Smith. I'd say:

F. E. Smith, 1st Earl of Birkenhead [pause] and I have very little in common. F.E. took silk at thirty-five, became Lord Chancellor at forty-seven, and was dead at fifty-eight, largely through drink. None of these things have I achieved. Nor was I, as he was, the Vinerian Law Scholar, Solicitor General, Attorney General and Secretary of State for India.

But the time came when, chatting to the students after one such dinner, to my astonishment I found that not one of them had ever previously even heard of F. E. Smith.

I then thought to substitute for F. E. Smith another legal legend, Rufus Isaacs, 1st Marquess of Reading, his career being perhaps even more remarkable than F.E.'s. Hammered on the Stock Exchange in his twenties, later closely associated with the Marconi scandal, Isaacs enjoyed immense success at the Bar, took silk at thirty-seven, became successively Solicitor General, Attorney General, Lord Chief Justice of England, Viceroy of

India and, finally, Foreign Secretary. He was, for good measure, and remains, the only commoner since the Duke of Wellington to be raised to the rank of Marquess.

Later, however, chatting to a similar group of students after another law dinner, I found (as perhaps readers will already have guessed) that Rufus Isaacs was no more of a name to them than F.E. had been. The fact was that these legendary figures – and others like them (Edward Marshall Hall, Edward Carson, Patrick Hastings, Edward Clarke, Norman Birkett, Hartley Shawcross) were certainly not legends to them. One or two of these names might ring a bell, but only in some narrow context – Birkett or Shawcross, say, because of their part in the Nuremberg trials; Carson and Clarke for, respectively, prosecuting and defending Oscar Wilde. Really one has to jump forward to the era of George Carman or even Michael Mansfield (hardly comparable figures) before alighting on a name recognised by the general public today. And who today, save perhaps David Pannick, could currently hope to be regarded as a household name?

I confess to finding all this deeply disheartening. It was in the celebrated biographies of legal giants past that I myself first recognised the drama and romance (what Tom Bingham once called the magic) of life at the Bar. For many of my generation, legal biographers like H. Montgomery Hyde and Edward Marjoribanks were themselves names to conjure with, let alone their subjects. Not only did such books capture our imagination and fire our ambitions, they described much about the Bar's ethos and style.

They were also (indeed, to my mind, still are) rattling good reads: after all, it is not in every era that careers such as those I have mentioned are forged. The closest equivalent of such books today are surely those of Thomas Grant KC, notably his compelling

Court Number One: The Old Bailey Trials that Defined Modern Britain, and his enthralling biographies of Jeremy Hutchinson and Sydney Kentridge (*The Mandela Brief*, an account of Kentridge's practice during South Africa's apartheid years).

Enough of all that: my readers may begin to think me guilty of pure nostalgia. Really, though, I am not. I am striving rather to persuade my younger readers, particularly anyone contemplating life at the Bar, to read the better legal biographies. Certainly I can think of no better way of learning something of the history of this great profession and of the towering figures who used to grace it.

◆

BEFORE, HOWEVER, saying a final farewell to Rufus Isaacs, I cannot resist a tail-piece to record how he, followed by his son, founded what eventually became my own chambers at 2 Garden Court (now re-created as 39 Essex Chambers). Rufus, before even he was called to the Bar, with astonishing self-confidence took chambers for himself at 1 Garden Court. As shown, however, by the Middle Temple's tenancy records, by 1907 he had moved to 2 Garden Court and there, in 1913, he was joined by his newly called, twenty-three-year-old son, Gerald (Lord Erleigh as he became in 1917 before finally succeeding his father as the 2nd Marquess of Reading in 1935).

Clear it is that the 2nd Marquess prospered greatly in his professional life, dying in 1960 at the age of seventy, laden with honours: GCMG, CBE, MC, PC, QC. In the 1950s he had been a Foreign Office minister. Whether his silk was granted for parliamentary reasons or for his practice I do not know.

But before those years of success comes a story I have long relished about Gerald's early approach to the Bar. In telling it I should at once acknowledge that it is entirely unconfirmed hearsay (related by Chambers elders down the years), mere gossip. Not that I object to gossip. On the contrary, I subscribe to the adage: "I don't like idle gossip; I like to keep it moving!"

At all events the story is that in his earliest days at the Bar Gerald had been above all a socialite. He was, of course, a highly eligible young man and doubtless much in demand in society. It was thus his principal concern that the Bar should not be allowed to interfere with his social life: in particular its demands should not extend beyond the hour when he would need to return home to bathe and change into a white tie. So it was, rumour had it, that if by ill chance he was last in the list at some outlying court, or for some other reason a late sitting seemed inevitable, out would come his cheque book and he would enquire as to what the claimant would take in settlement and of course as to both sides' costs.

I do hope the story is true, at least of one or two occasions. Indeed I personally would regard it as greatly to the young man's credit, demonstrating an attractively carefree and patrician attitude to life before the long years of danger and responsibility ahead. This after all was just before the outbreak of the Great War, a war in which, it will be remembered, Gerald won an MC. Certainly I used to tell this tale with no thought that it might be regarded as inconsistent with my boasts of Chambers' distinguished history.

Of course I recognise that few new tenants these days could afford to behave quite as the young 2nd Marquess is said to have done and, indeed, it may be doubted if such an approach today would enhance one's prospects of a successful future at the Bar. But I would be disappointed, indeed saddened, if the young today would on that account regret rather than relish the inclusion of the 2nd Marquess amongst their illustrious forebears in Chambers.

CHAPTER 10

The Chagossians

T HIS CHAPTER is prompted by Philippe Sands's enthralling
new book about the Chagossians, *The Last Colony*. It is the story,
compellingly told, of Britain's expulsion of the native population
from the Chagos Islands in the mid 1960s, essentially to allow the
United States to establish a military base on Diego Garcia, and it
tells too of the islanders' persistent subsequent efforts to return.

Only after decades of litigation was it finally decided in 2019
by the International Court of Justice in The Hague that the
expulsion had been unlawful. It had violated UN resolution 1514
guaranteeing self-determination and territorial integrity. It was
held, in short, that Britain had had no right in 1965 to establish the
Chagos Islands as a new colony, British Indian Ocean Territory
(BIOT), at which time the archipelago already belonged to
Mauritius, itself then a British colony. When in 1968 Mauritius
gained independence, the islands remained part of it.

I have maintained a considerable interest in all this for a very
particular reason. One of the Chagossians' several earlier avenues
of litigation had ended in a decision of the House of Lords in
2008 in the case of Bancoult. This was essentially an irrationality
challenge to a 2004 order extinguishing, purportedly on grounds

of national security, an earlier immigration ordinance permitting the Chagossians to return to all their islands except for Diego Garcia. The House of Lords, reversing the Court of Appeal's decision, rejected the challenge by a bare majority of three (Lords Hoffmann, Rodger and Carswell) to two (Lords Bingham and Mance). The European Court of Human Rights (ECtHR) in Strasbourg in turn then rejected the Chagossians' claim, but on the explicit basis that Britain's occupation of the islands was lawful under international law, a premise, as already stated, later found false.

Meantime, however, I had on occasions wondered whether possibly I myself had played a part in the Chagossians' 2008 defeat. Originally I was one of the five Law Lords assigned to the appeal. I had, however, asked to be released from the case, having promised to be elsewhere that day, a commitment long since notified to the court. True, the commitment was merely to present the prizes at the well-known charity Crimestoppers' annual golf day. But I had reneged on the very same commitment the previous year when that too had clashed with an appeal hearing and I didn't feel I could properly let Crimestoppers down again. (This was, I may say, the only occasion I had ever made myself unavailable for a court hearing and it proved to be a mistake which I never repeated.)

I cannot of course say whether my absence made the slightest difference to the outcome. I do not know who replaced me in the committee's constitution nor, not having heard the arguments, what conclusion I personally would have arrived at. It would, of course, only have affected the result if I was in fact replaced by one of the majority and had I in the event come to a different view. I later found the judgments both of the majority and the minority highly persuasive, sympathy for the Chagossians and scepticism as to the government's case being by no means confined to the latter.

Now, of course, the Chagossians have happily won their case to be allowed back to their islands. But regrettably the government still refuses to give effect to this ruling, and in any event the 2008 decision plainly cost them many further years of exile for which Britain itself cannot escape responsibility.

I shall end this perhaps somewhat inconsequential chapter by way of another instance of a House of Lords appeal committee having to be changed through the unavailability of one of its members. This absence, however, was for an altogether better reason and proved of altogether greater significance. I am speaking of the Senior Law Lord, Lord Browne-Wilkinson's absence from the constitution of the committee hearing the first of what became a series of Lords' hearings in the Pinochet case.

This case concerned Spain's application to extradite Chile's erstwhile dictator, General Pinochet, from the U.K. during a visit here. Lord Browne-Wilkinson was unavailable because he was attending the ceremonial opening of the new ECtHR building in Strasbourg and, as was customary in those days, he was replaced by the next senior available Law Lord, Lord Hoffmann as it happened. The rest, as they say, is history, at least it is for lawyers, the only people likely to be interested in this generally unrecognised quirk of fate. For those who do not already know the unusual course the Lords appeal took, what follows is, I hope, sufficient.

A second, fresh panel of Law Lords, presided over by Lord Browne-Wilkinson, set aside the Lords' original decision (3:2 had been in favour of extradition) on the ground of apparent bias, Lord Hoffmann's wife having an association with Amnesty

International, a party intervening in the proceedings. At that point a third, again wholly fresh, panel had to be assembled (with some difficulty) to re-hear the appeal, this panel too in the event deciding in favour of extradition, albeit for trial on a narrower basis than had originally been ordered.

ॐ

TO THIS END PIECE I cannot now resist adding, self-indulgently I acknowledge, a further footnote. It so happened that the very final instalment of this long-running Pinochet litigation took place in the Divisional Court where I myself was presiding. The Home Secretary was then about to refuse extradition (just finally held lawful) on medical grounds, and Spain and Belgium were seeking a court order requiring him first to disclose to them the joint opinion of a group of distinguished medical experts certifying the General's unfitness to stand trial.

Despite the forceful advocacy of Jonathan Sumption QC (whom I well recall complaining, probably with justification, that I was being grossly unfair to his arguments), we made the disclosure order – on the express basis that the medical report would be treated with the utmost confidentiality and be shown only to a handful of senior officials. Regrettably, however, within an hour of the judgment being given, the news-stands were selling evening papers carrying verbatim extracts from the report.

Later events, of course, suggested that perhaps after all the doctors had been at least partially duped. My own involvement in the Pinochet saga, however, can hardly be regarded as a triumph.

CHAPTER 11

Launching Beloff

Michael Beloff's memoir, MJBQC: A Life Within and Without the Law *was published in April 2022. He had asked me to give the introductory speech at the launch in Gray's Inn (to be followed by Lord Justice Rabinder Singh).*

WHEN I asked Michael what sort of an introduction he was looking for at this launch, he referred me to David Neuberger's encomium on the back of the dust jacket which indeed in a few well-chosen words – ignoring, *pace* the proofreader, a superfluous "that" – admirably captures the essence of our memoirist.

Truly Michael has led a remarkable life, bestriding many different worlds: vast tracts of the law, academe, politics, sport, not to mention an active social life. He has been everywhere, seen everything, met everyone. The story, doubtless apocryphal, is told of Michael, lunching with an old friend, who suddenly starts looking under the table. Asked what he's lost, the friend replies: "Nothing," he was just making sure the table supports were sturdy enough to bear the weight of all the names being dropped upon it!

Small wonder the indexer obviously found difficulty in keeping up. But really it's a mistake to go, as so many of us do, straight to the index. Even if one's name is there, even indeed with multiple references, it's invariably a disappointment. How on earth, one wonders, could the author have been so stupid as to omit the one story we had hoped and expected to find, generally of course a story to one's own advantage.

I found Michael a daunting opponent in the few short years between his developing a leading public law practice, sometimes with a promising young white-wigged junior called Pannick (whatever happened to him?), and my own departure for the Bench. I once observed that his formidable advocacy was the product of a fertile mind, great oratorical skills and a rich use of language. These qualities are no less apparent in his prose. So too is what I had added, and he now quotes:

Every submission slips seamlessly into the next, parentheses are legion, and no sentence ever quite ends.

That made it difficult to note. Here, happily, it merely sweeps one along on an irresistible tide of reminiscence, reflection and anecdote, almost osmotically absorbing the many footnotes. The memoir is, of course, compelling, dazzling, breathless.

Wondering how best to convey its overall flavour, it struck me as if in a single work were to be found all three volumes of Chips Channon's *Diaries*, interspersed with all twelve volumes of Anthony Powell's *A Dance to the Music of Time*, the whole lavishly garnished with Wodehousian metaphor and simile. It is not a memoir to be devoured at a single sitting.

Michael has been the very model of a fashionable silk, the go-to advocate for any exciting, often groundbreaking, case. How he got through so much work in so many corners of the globe is quite remarkable. He must have an iron constitution, a prodigious work ethic, and boundless self-confidence, occasionally bordering, dare one say, on sheer chutzpah.

A while ago I took great delight in a grandson's school report commenting that he always seemed to find the twenty-fifth hour in every day. That, however, would have been wholly insufficient for Michael. He has needed at least the eighth day in every week and presumably too a Thatcherite ability to survive on just four or five hours' sleep a night.

Down the years endless accolades have been showered upon Michael in innumerable different contexts, a veritable avalanche of encomia. Not all of these, how shall I put this, have escaped mention in this memoir. Perhaps, however, as he suggests, I myself am to blame, having immodestly included in my own memoir a tribute from Tom Bingham, describing it as an unmissable opportunity to savour, cherish and broadcast such praise. And in fairness to Michael, the temptations for him have been altogether more acute. I should note too that he recounts not only his triumphs but also his occasional setbacks: his failure to win a prize fellowship at All Souls (*proxime accessit* in a year insufficiently distinguished to justify the usual second award); his being passed over in favour of Robert Carnwath for appointment as Revenue Junior; his narrowly missing a podium spot in an inter-Counties quarter-mile race, coming fourth, candidly adding that there *were* only four runners!

So Michael is really no Mr Toad.

But frankly all that is by the way. Here he has given us a vivid, fascinating account of a richly diverse life, full of interest, charm and wit. He could never bore us. Rather with this memoir he remains an ever loyal, ever loveable presence in our midst, continuing to light up our own comparatively humdrum lives.

By the by, buy the book: lest there appear in future a Bateman cartoon of The Lawyer Who Didn't!

Rabinder, over to you.

CHAPTER 12

Life's a Party

D OWN THE YEARS I've been to a great many excellent parties; and, indeed, as I like to think, given a few myself, though admittedly not for some while now.

Good parties come in all shapes and sizes, in myriad different settings, held for a whole variety of reasons. But every party has this in common: as the guests arrive and enter into the spirit of the occasion, it reaches a crescendo – of greetings and introductions, of noise, of gossip exchanged, of general enjoyment and exuberance.

And then, however long later, a corresponding diminuendo, as those attending begin seeking out the host to express their thanks and bid their farewells, before finally making their departures. The excitement and anticipation of the earlier phase draws to a close. The noise dwindles. People have ceased shouting. Laughter is muted. Bottles are no longer opened, glasses no longer filled. The canapés, earlier in circulation, have all now been consumed. Even the bowls of nuts and crisps are empty. There is not an olive to be seen. One has now the sense of an ending, of the chatter gradually dying away, of interest and expectation waning. The initial excitement has given way to contentment (or for some, maybe, disappointment).

Is life really so very different? Truly I think not.

After spending the last eighty-five years at just such a party, my own enthusiasm and expectations by this point have undoubtedly declined. It is, surely, hardly surprising that one's earlier feelings of excitement have been replaced rather by contentment (in my case certainly not disappointment). Frankly, I have had my share of the canapés (indeed, rather more than my share). My glass has been filled quite often enough. My appetite for gossip is, of course, inexhaustible; but, that said, it is difficult to believe there remains much left that could still surprise, let alone shock, me. And, altogether less inexhaustible, alas, are my energy levels: my ability to continue for long to stand and wander around, intermingling with others whom I can no longer always recognise and whose remarks nowadays I catch with only variable success. How enormously welcome a sofa would be. Not to mention a reduction in the noise level.

Really, however, this long into the event, with drink and sheer tiredness beginning to take their toll not only of my own contribution to the occasion but indeed of everyone's ability to keep the party spirit going, the imperative has become to avoid being the last to leave. One has met, or now sadly missed, those one was keen to meet; chatted to those that one knew. Most of one's close friends have already departed. And one really rather envies their having become able at last to loosen their ties, to relax in their behaviour and finally reach the peace and quiet of home.

It has all been the greatest fun. But, goodness me, after such a very protracted outing, how hugely appealing is now the prospect of home and a good long sleep. Thanks indeed to all my hosts and fellow guests. Fond farewells to each one of you. And, at long last, a heartfelt goodnight to everyone.

CHAPTER 13

Lights Out

I HONESTLY do not fear death, though naturally would prefer it to be quick and painless. But I am appalled at the prospect of a protracted old age, becoming, as logically one must, ever more disabled and debilitated, the limitations and afflictions multiplying with each passing year. Pityingly we watch the process of inexorable decline affecting the great majority of the aged amongst us.

Each of us will one day die. And few surely would wish it otherwise. So why, oh why, does almost everyone seem to want to postpone that inevitability as long as possible? Do the elderly not realise that, whatever adverse effect ageing is already having upon their general powers and faculties, diminishing their overall quality and enjoyment of life, realistically this can only increase? Do they not appreciate that the nation's health and care resources are already stretched to breaking point? Surely it makes no sense at all to devote ever more of these to the creation of an ever-growing population of ever-older, ever less productive, ever more enfeebled elders. Ours is an already overpopulated world. By all means let us work strenuously to maximise the health and happiness, the general well-being, of those not yet elderly. But those of us like me, now eighty-five, who have long since had their years in the sun, the lawyers their day in court, should surely now step aside – accept rather than fight their end – once the opportunity arises. And not only for the sake of those following on, those whose turn it now is for a spell in the sun, but also for their own sakes, to pre-empt the increasing degrees of disability and decay that inevitably lie ahead. I am not here advocating suicide, rather a cessation of life-prolonging treatment.

I view all this admittedly from a firmly atheistic standpoint, giving no weight to what the religious would regard as the sanctity of life. I mean, of course, human life as opposed to a dog's or cat's life which all would readily end if they thought it to be in the animal's best interests – or, for that matter, a cow's or sheep's life, if intended for consumption. Naturally I recognise that even the religious disavow any "need to strive officiously to keep alive". But my point goes altogether further and wider than this: I question why we are so indulgent towards the increasingly elderly, so inappropriately overgenerous as I would suggest we are in our allocation to them of every precious resource. In the same way, I regret rather than admire the relentless efforts of those reaching ever closer towards their end to delay it for yet longer.

In times now regrettably past, pneumonia was always said to be the "old people's friend". "Friend" note, not "enemy". It was widely thought a kindness to spare those affected the rigours of further ageing.

Why, I am tempted to ask, should it be thought right to deny to the aged this God-given means of release and suppose instead that mankind is duty-bound rather to continue searching for ever-cleverer ways of lengthening humanity's life span?

How, I wonder, in their hearts, do the bishops, the doctors, the scientists, those allocating resources in the Department of Health, view the prospect of ever-lengthening life?

As each common killer – cancers and heart disease perhaps nowadays the closest equivalents of pneumonia in times past – succumbs gradually to research and successful treatment, are we to grow ever older? Should we indeed be looking forward to a time when we may enjoy the benefits of spare-part surgery? Or is the whole problem of ageing soon to be averted by new drugs and treatments that will actually reverse the ageing process? Will there eventually come a point at which all illnesses are curable, all deaths preventable? Are we not to be allowed to depart this earth, to call it a day?

Irreligious though I am, I too regard life as a gift. But not a gift from God, rather from nature, or perhaps from one's parents or, and this is what I really feel, a gift from all those who contribute to its potential for happiness and fulfilment. In my own case that has been above all my wife and family. But it includes too the ever-widening circle of one's friends and colleagues who, to use the party analogy I elaborated in the last chapter, "Life's a Party", made the party for me such fun.

That is the gift for which I am so truly grateful. But the time must surely come when eventually the fun ends and one wants to leave the party: Life has become more trouble than it's worth and so, frankly, have you. And of course leave it you can. Nobody says we've thrown this party for you, we'll go on providing food and shelter, so we're going to lock the door and keep you here. Is it really asking too much of the donor of the gift of life, as we ask of our host when leaving a party, please open the door and let us out? For the life of me (not, I hope, an inappropriate expression in this context) I cannot believe it is. Rather let us say: Heaven forfend.

Index

Page numbers in red refer to illustrations
Entries with asterisks also feature in *Playing off the Roof & Other Stories*